"It is not good that man should be alone; I will make him a helper comparable to him. Love one another; as I have loved you. Let all that you do be done with love."

God, CEO of heaven and earth
Genesis 2:18 (NKJV); John 13:34 (NKJV);
1 Corinthians 16:14 (NKJV)

D0920910

Published by Tate Publishing & Enterprises, LLC
127 E. Trade Center Terrace | Mustang, Oklahoma 73064 USA
1.888.361.9473 | www.tatepublishing.com

Tate Publishing is committed to excellence in the publishing industry. The company reflects the philosophy established by the founders, based on Psalm 68:11,
"The Lord gave the word and great was the company of those who published it."

Book design copyright © 2008 by Tate Publishing, LLC. All rights reserved.
Cover design by Kandi Evans, Interior design by Lance Waldrop

Published in the United States of America

ISBN: 978-1-60696-552-8
1. Chr.Liv.:Relationships:Love/Marr.
2. Chr.Liv:Prac.Life:Enc&LayCouns
08.08.22

Kissing
and Cooking

A Recipe To Add *Spice and Romance*
To Your Marriage

For Couples

Kim Reutzel

TATE PUBLISHING & *Enterprises*

Dedication

I would like to dedicate this book to my husband, without whom I wouldn't have had any material to write about. But most of all, for all the laughs and love you surprise me with daily! I love you very much. A special dedication is given to Tess for the hours she spent reviewing this book and setting me on the right track. You're the best daughter a mother could dream of. To my mom and dad, who have always cheered me on and encouraged me. Last but not least, to my son and daughter-in-law, Tad and Karly, and my beautiful granddaughter, Hailee. I love you all very much. I pray that God my bless each and every one of you and make all your dreams come true. Thank you for being a part of my dreams.

Acknowledgments

This book would have not been possible without my good friends Becky and Carla. You both have been such a great encouragement to me; I can't even begin to put down into words what you have meant to me. Your love and your "you can do its" were not taken lightly. Thanks, Becky, for being my spell check. Also, thank you, Deb, for always being there for me no matter what I had going on. I love all my family very much. You have each touched my life in many different ways. I would also like to thank Dr. Phyllis Arno for reviewing my book and giving me the spiritual guidance I so much needed. You are a beautiful, Godly woman who has blessed many lives. Lastly, I would like to thank my Heavenly Father. You are my strength and shield, and I wouldn't have been able to do it without Your loving words to encourage me from Holy Scripture.

Table of Contents

17 How was Kissing and Cooking Stirred up?

25 Different as a Chili Pepper and a Vanilla Bean

26 *You need to be happy first*

28 *Just be you*

29 *The Marriage Team*

30 *Know your differences*

35 *Our Family Differences*

37 *Differences are normal and good*

38 *We are all different, yet the same*

39 Only Loving Thoughts of You, Right?

40 *Are your thoughts important?*

42 *Pay attention to your body*

46 *Make your yes be yes, and your no be no!*

49 *Stopping wrong thinking stops wrong words and actions*

50 *Don't reason something wrong into something right*

52 *Be motivated to think right thoughts*

53 *Using Self-Control to Control Thoughts*

55 *Filter your thoughts*

56 *What do you want to happen?*

57 *Make a choice to think good thoughts*

61 *Do you do what you think you do?*

63 *Thoughts are definitely important*

65 <u>We Ordered Caviar, Where is the Caviar?</u>

66 *The honeymoon feeling*

67 *What is love?*

68 *Realize the world is not what it seems to be*

70 *It's not always fifty/fifty*

71 *What is not realistic in a relationship?*

73   Let's Spend the Night Together - Kissing!

73   *Are you nourishing your marriage?*

76   *Plan special times together*

77   *Is there a secret to a happy marriage?*

77   *Respect each other's interests*

79   *Have some interests of your own also*

80   *What you put time into can be great*

83   Isn't Kissing Communicating?

83   *Communication, communication, communication!*

85   *What is communication?*

86   *More is being said than what comes out of your mouth*

87   *Strengthen your communication*

89   *Who do you dream to be?*

91   *Communicate straight from the heart*

92   *What are your spouse's emotional needs?*

93   *Your attitudes matters*

94 *Do you tell others what to do or ask for their help?*

96 *Practice good communication skills*

99 <u>Let's Kiss and Make up!</u>

100 *Conflict is inevitable; compromise is a choice*

101 *Resolve conflicts like a best ballgame of golf*

102 *Using the tool and how to get to a compromise*

110 *Throwing in the Towel*

111 *Things to Keep in Mind*

115 <u>Love Me Tenderly</u>

116 *What is love?*

119 *Considerations for Love in a Marriage*

120 *Then what is love in a marriage?*

121 *Final Thoughts*

122 <u>Menu One</u>
     *Almond chicken crescent entrée, flavored orange greens,
     and glazed apple roll-ups*

134 <u>Menu Two</u>
Sauteed vegetables with steak, peppered provolone bread, and heart-shaped ice-cream sandwiches

142 <u>Menu Three</u>
Sweetened popcorn and a romantic movie

148 <u>Menu Four</u>
Creamy mushroom-filled ravioli with shrimp, sweetened chilled spinach, and orange sherbet

158 <u>Menu Five</u>
Sunset eggs benedict and fresh-fruit delight

166 <u>Menu Six</u>
Philly steak delight, heavenly potatoes, chilled tomato salad, and chocolate mint ice cream

176 <u>Menu Seven</u>
Creamy chicken enchiladas, crispy iceberg salad, and grilled chocolate tortillas

186 <u>Menu Eight</u>
Sunny island kabobs, kiwi surprise, and buttery garlic bread

196 <u>Menu Nine</u>
Tomato dip with chips, cheesy zucchini with rice, and banana creamed pie

204 <u>Menu Ten</u>
Cheesy chicken manicotti, sweet slaw, and seasoned custard

214 <u>Menu Eleven</u>
Cheese and crackers, picnic turkey wraps, and creamy marshmallow and strawberries

222 <u>Menu Twelve</u>
Rolled lasagna with veggies, french baguette, creamy cucumbers over spinach, and chilled chocolate fudge pie

How was Kissing and Cooking Stirred up?

The news that four couples in our small little collection of towns had split up, along with the gossip that affairs were the culprit, sent shivers down my spine. What was I to do to keep this phenomenon from visiting my own marriage of twenty-five years? It is everywhere we look, in the television shows we sit down to relax with each night, the movies we pay to see, and our nightly news. The latest report I heard was that around fifty percent of marriages will end in divorce. What a trickle down effect this has on our neighborhoods, communities, and country. The cost to our country and families is just too high to bear, not only financially but also emotionally. The effect it has is too enormous to sit around and watch it destroy one family after another.

Having earned a master's degree in clinical

Christian counseling, and as the president and pastoral counselor for Inspiration for Women Ministries, a non-profit ministry, I had the heavenly drive and faith that something could slow down this injustice effecting so many of our lives. God had sent many troubled marriages to my counseling office, so I heard firsthand the real emotional hurt and conflict divorce caused. What was making so may people who were once in love say, "The loves gone," or worse yet that they think maybe they were never really in love? I prayed, *What can I do? How can I help?*

For some reason this news hit me to the core. What had kept my marriage together when it had every reason to fail? I have to admit my teen years were very adventurous; I could have been the national spokesperson for the wild child. At age eighteen I was unwed and expecting a baby. Plans were made to hurry a wedding, and the "I dos" were said. Five months later we welcomed our precious little baby girl, and our wonderful son followed two and a half years later. I look back now and think, *Life has just happened.*

But why had we beaten the odds when so many unions that seemed to be the storybook marriages had failed? It wasn't because our marriage had not faced challenges. We had many. But we are still together and, I would have to add, surprisingly happy. Even so, the news about all these broken marriages, along with the miserable couples I counseled, tugged deep inside my soul. I made a commitment that I would not take my marriage for granted and it would always be nurtured with special care, commitment, and God's loving grace. As I thought more about it, I realized maybe we had never taken our marriage for granted and had really worked on it. As problems arose we made adjustments to protect what we had. Yet it was not always easy and sometimes seemed impossible, like trying to push a car up a hill while someone has the brake pressed down.

I definitely had an uneasy feeling, as we are approaching another milestone in our marriage. We are empty nesters and middle agers at the same time! Thoughts ran through my mind. *It's just you and me, babe!* How was I going to make sure this aging stud of mine was going to have eyes for only me as I rooted yet another gray hair? *Ouch!*

As I sat and watched one of my favorite cooking shows, solutions to keep our marriage spicy started to dance in my head. Could we cook together? Wait, this macho man of mine, whose specialty is fried eggs dripping with butter, would cook with me? What was I thinking? Not only that, but I had to be honest with my own cooking abilities. A domestic goddess I am not! It would take an act of God for this fantasy to happen. I realized I had to think of something to entice him (or should I say trick him into it). I felt we needed something to keep our relationship interesting or maybe even a little on the steamy side and thought that this may be the answer. Just then, lighting struck. *Kissing and Cooking*…this will get his attention! So I planned our first night of cooking. I told him I would make sure the cooking of his favorite meal (lasagna) would get done, and his job was to make sure plenty of kissing would get done. *Hmmm, I think he's going for it.*

The day of our *Kissing and Cooking* date night came, and we teased each other throughout the day not to get too tired because tonight was the night! I had bought a special beverage, along with all the ingredients and gave him special vegetable chopping jobs to prepare the lasagna. All of a sudden I thought I was in the kitchen with a professional chef, teasing me with the spice of a character in a romance novel. Things seemed to be getting a little hot in the kitchen, and it wasn't coming from the oven this time. I had planned some special questions for us to talk about that would spark emotional and physical intimacy— and it worked! The questions were designed to go outside our normal everyday conversations. We both learned some new and interesting things about each other that night and left that evening having a lot of fun. But even more importantly, we left with a newfound understanding and bond to each other.

The next day I reflected on the fun experience we had and realized that if it worked for us, it could work for others also. As I planned how this could help others, we joked that this could be the next big cooking show, but my husband teased: it might be better suited for late night! All kidding aside, it really helped our relationship and brought some newfound romance into it. I really believe, as a counselor, wife, and a human being just wanting to have a little fun, this can honestly benefit other couples.

So, I was armed with a fun date night idea that would be easy for couples to implement in their busy lives, but found it necessary to get to the nitty-gritty of what really keeps a relationship fun and spontaneous this day and age.

It is obvious the planning is not done after the wedding is over. Families hire wedding planners to help them plan a successful wedding. It has been said, "Families that play together, stay together." And this book starts with the core members: you, the *parents*. Every marriage would be helped if it had a marriage planner; use my book as your personal marriage planner to help with the skills that can lead you to a wonderful and lasting married life together.

It doesn't matter if you are soon-to-be married, have been married forty days or forty years, are married to a gourmet chef or a motor head, whether you are whole- or half-heartedly co-existing, contemplating divorce, or are on your third marriage; use the skills in this book for a better future. This is not a book to make anyone feel guilty or ashamed. This book is about forgiving yourself and others for past mistakes and living a life of peace and love with the one God has given you to share your life with. It is not about being able to do everything in your marriage perfectly or without a few struggles. My subconscious and my daughter have told me a time or two that I needed to go back and read what I wrote in my own book.

After much prayer, biblical research, and soul-searching, I have come up with seven recommendations that can spice up any relationship. These are things I have used in my marriage and at my counseling office, and they really seem to work. These are more than just helpful hints of what you need to do to maintain your relationship; they also give you an outlet to work on your relationship in a way that is exciting and non-confrontational. I'm not attempting to fill your head with knowledge and give you a "do this" list, but am providing you the avenue through *Kissing and Cooking* to advance your life and your family's life. Would you like to understand your mate on a whole new level?

If so, roll up your sleeves, smack your lips, tickle your funny bone, and have some fun with the person God has placed in your life through *Kissing and Cooking for Couples*. Designed by a concerned, imperfect, God fearing, *marriage planner* with the heart to help all of God's people who would like to spice up their own relationships.

Different as a Chili Pepper and a Vanilla Bean

When Sara and Peter were dating, they giggled and played with each other. Love was filling the air. They could not see themselves spending their lives with anyone else. She would go golfing with him, and he went shopping with her, anything to spend precious time together. They spent long nights talking about all their hopes and dreams. The wedding was planned, with beautiful flowers placed perfectly. Everything was a dream come true right down to the large tiered wedding cake flowing with lilies. She said her vows with joyful tears rolling down her cheeks. Then they danced under the sparkling stars until the evening was spent. It was a wonderful start to their dreams of a loving life together. Now, three years later, they could hardly do anything together anymore. She wondered what had happened to their dreamy start. She no longer wanted to go golfing with him, and he didn't shop with her. Sara felt alone and unhappy and felt he didn't care. Thoughts that she had made a mistake kept fogging her mind. She spent lonely nights alone in the bedroom reading, with tears falling down her cheeks. How had she gotten to such a point of despair? What would they need to do to enjoy each other's company? She wondered, what could she do to change the way she felt?

You need to be happy first!

Before you can be a happy person in a relationship, you must first be a happy person within yourself. One of the most freeing things I had happen to me was to understand my temperament through the use of *Creation Therapy*, developed by Drs. Phyllis and Richard Arno and marketed through the *Sarasota Academy of Christian Counseling*. It helped me be free to be me. I had been trying to fit into what I *thought* the world and the Christian community said was normal behavior. What a hard situation to be in; it is really hard to be someone else. You are the best person to be who God created you to be! So stop trying to fit into some manmade mold you have created for yourself. The psalmist's words recorded this.

> You made all the delicate, inner parts of my body and knit me together in my mother's womb. Thank you for making me so wonderfully complex! Your workmanship is marvelous—and how well I know it. You watched me as I was being formed in utter seclusion, as I was woven together in the dark of the womb. You saw me before I was born. Every day of my life was recorded in your book. Every moment was laid out before a single day had passed.
>
> Psalm 139:13–16 (NLT)

God created my inmost being. Everything about me was written before I was born. Wow! In our humanness, it's sometimes hard to understand God's greatness and ability!

The following is a fictional story I heard somewhere that touched my heart. After Dave died he was waiting at the heavenly gates for his turn to enter. Finally, when it was his turn, Jesus walked up to him and gave him a big hug and asked him if he would like a tour of heaven. Dave was delighted at this request. As they started on their walk, Jesus asked him about a few events that had happened in his life and how he had handled them. After they had been talking for a while, Jesus stopped and looked Dave straight in the eyes. With loving concern he said, "My Father was wondering, why wasn't it okay to just be Dave?"

Just be you.

We are all misled into thinking there is some normalcy in character out there to try to achieve. And our feelings of good or bad self-esteem stem from whether we feel we are normal or whether everyone else is normal and we are not. One of the best things you can do to strengthen yourself and your relationship is to decide it is okay to be the person God made you to be. He has a special purpose for each one of us and has given us special traits to fulfill His will in our lives. We are not a surprise to God. The Bible verifies this, "For we are His workmanship, created in Christ Jesus for good works, which God prepared beforehand that we should walk in them" (Ephesians 2:10, NKJV).

The Marriage Team

We all look different, and moreover, we definitely think, talk, act, and dream differently. We all were born for special reasons and were provided with different abilities to accomplish them. Look at your differences as an extension of who you and your spouse can be together!

In a sports team it is important that each player has and knows his or her own strengths to fulfill a special position on the team. Each player's strength put together with the other players' strengths will make a good team; where one has a weakness, another can be strong.

Similarly, in a marriage, each person is different, and each spouse has his or her own strengths and weaknesses. In your marriage relationship, you will each have your own special strengths, which when respected by the other, can be used to develop a great *marriage team*. Always remember, you are teammates and not on opposing teams. Traditionally you are taught to *encourage* your own team and try to make the other team stumble. A point to remember is that you gain points and build your partner up for a better performance by pointing out his strengths, not his weaknesses. So embrace your differences as a strength, and help each other develop the special personal characteristics that will help you be a better team together than if you were playing in the game of life separately. Are you a teammate any team would be proud to call its own?

Another point to remember is a good teammate is also your best cheerleader, not your stumbling block. Encourage, encourage, and encourage more!

Know your differences.

How do you find your differences? How can you build on each other's strengths and work on your weaknesses? As I said previously, for me it was through *Creation Therapy*, using the Arno Profile

System profile (A.P.S.), which I use in my counseling office. By answering a few quick questions, a clinical report is developed. This report will give you your personal temperament or your "temperament blends," which then are explained to you by a specially trained individual. This report will explain your God-given temperament very thoroughly to help you understand why you act the way you do. Within each temperament there are strengths and weakness to build on and be cautious of. Knowing your temperament frees you to be you and encourages you to work on your weaknesses. In couples therapy it is a wonderful tool because the couples are able to learn about their specific differences and understand why they do what they do and how they can help each other's needs. Even if your differences are not as different as a chili pepper and a vanilla bean, you still will benefit by understanding each other better.

How better to explain this than to use Del, my husband, and me as an example. (He will love me for this, I'm sure!) I will leave the technical terms out. I am an extreme people person, and he relates better to tasks. So let's just say he's a worker and I'm a player. He needs time to think things through, and I am very spontaneous. My spontaneity has gotten me into trouble with Del a few times in my life. I guess he likes his clothes in their drawer so he has something to wear to work, and for some reason he would like some meat and potatoes on the table after fourteen hours of work. I like to spend time with my friends, and this has caused a few heated disagreements in our relationship.

Learning my temperament was very helpful. I found that I had a compulsive need to be around people, and this was affecting my responsibilities. I needed to take time to think things through before I just jumped in a car to go somewhere. I found through Del's test that it was very important to him that I had these things done for him, because one of his temperament needs was to have things orderly. He also showed love by doing things for me to make my life easier. By not responding to his needs, I caused him stress, which in return caused me stress.

As Del started to understand this part of my temperament, he realized it caused me stress when I was not around people for long periods of time. Now he doesn't get worked up when I want to have lunch with friends. We now call it "my hobby." Recognizing that this was a temperament weakness of mine, I tried harder to fulfill my responsibilities, and in doing this it caused more peace at home. I have also found other things I can do to help me feel comfortable without being with people all the time. Listening to a radio or reading books can eliminate the stress I felt when alone. Recognizing this, I can now spend long periods alone, and I even enjoy myself. I needed to find a balance within my temperament to experience the peace that could follow.

However, it was important to realize God placed this need in me so I could do what he had planned for my life. I wouldn't be able to counsel or speak without being a people person. I just needed to recognize it and get it into balance so it didn't cause stress in my life or my loved one's life. In God's Word it says, "…I will never leave you or forsake you" (Hebrews 13:5, NKJV). This Scripture reminds me I am truly never alone anyway.

The first step in finding this peace is recognizing you and your spouse each have different needs and then finding out what they are and making changes to suit you both. If something is causing problems in your marriage, you are probably fulfilling your temperament needs in an unhealthy way. Understanding your differences and making a few adjustments will make a world of difference. It is not about being controlling or bossy; it's about meeting each other's temperament needs with humility and sacrificing for each other. When your partner's needs are met, it is easier for him or her to respond with love to your needs. And that is how the circle of love continues to go around and around. So if he needs to add a little excitement into his life, live it up with him. Then ask him to relax with you the following day. Personal happiness grows with a little giving and taking in your relationship.

Remember, the Golden Rule never tarnishes. I have expanded the Golden Rule for marriages. "Do unto your spouse what you would have them do unto you. Expect less done unto you than you do unto your spouse, because we are all sinful and selfish by nature." Thank you, Jesus, for covering our humanness with Your death on the cross! Help us to forgive and forget others' shortcomings like You have forgiven and forgotten our shortcomings.

Our Family Differences

I'm sure many of you have experienced these words, "My parents did it this way, so we should do it this way." The way you were raised has a lot to do with who you are today and what you bring into the marriage. However, it is not an excuse to fail to compromise or to continue in bad behavior when it is making your spouse miserable.

> No, dear brothers and sisters, I am still not all I should be, but I am focusing all my energies on this one thing: Forgetting the past and looking forward to what lies ahead, I strain to reach the end of the race and receive the prize for which God, through Christ Jesus, is calling us up to heaven.
>
> Philippians 3:13–14 (NLT)

This passage does not just say forgetting will just happen; it says you must strain for the prize. Therefore it will be work! You have no control over the way you were brought up, but you can make choices that will change the effect it has on you and how you will let it affect your family and future. The Word says, "Delight yourself also in the LORD, And He shall give you the desires of your heart" (Psalm 37:4, NKJV). You are not alone! When you commit to Him, your desires are His desires, and He will help you fulfill His will in your life. His Word also says you will need to leave your mother and father. "Therefore a man shall leave his father and mother and be joined to his wife, and they shall become one flesh" (Genesis 2:24, NKJV). The oneness is hard! Just like your parents and others had to discover a system that worked between them, you will too. In a marriage it is important to remember, there is more than one way to get the same result. Simple, *right?* About as simple as giving birth to an elephant! The following are a few ways to resolve differences of opinion: one time do it your way, and the next do it your spouse's way. Flip a coin, give and take; I'll do this your way if I can do this other thing my way. Sometimes you have to swallow your pride and humble yourself and decide your spouse's way is better. It may feel like you're swallowing something as large as a watermelon, but you can do it. Believe me. I know.

Your family is now your spouse and children;

everyone else is your relatives. Hmm, that can put a different picture on things, can't it? Make a commitment to your family and love your relatives from enough distance to have a healthy relationship with your spouse. And that does mean sometimes you will have to do things a different way than you have been taught.

Differences are normal and good.

Being different and having different ideas or ways than your spouse only means you have two different people in a normal relationship. Don't read too much into it. And definitely don't compare your relationship to what you believe you see in other couples' relationships. I like to compare what we see in others to a duck floating on top of a pond. They appear to be so peaceful, sunning and feeding themselves. But when you look under the water, their feet are going a mile a minute. Things don't always appear as they are on the outside. We can all put a good front on when we need to. But the truth is, all couples have differences and disagreements. Give your marriage the compassion and understanding it needs to grow and flourish.

We are all different, yet the same.

After saying all this about how different we are, I have to say we are still the same in some ways. We all want to be loved—some by a few and some by many. We all make mistakes—some hurt us, and some hurt others. We all have dreams—some big, some small. And we all truly just want peace.

A marriage is about being one. So when you help your spouse, love, forgive, dream, and have peace, you are really helping yourself.

A happy spouse is a happy you!!

Only Loving Thoughts of You. Right?

He is always late getting home—will he ever be dependable? What could he possibly be doing out this late? I saw how he looked at Pam the other night; could he be meeting her? Or has he run his car into the ditch and it flipped over on top of him? I'd like to place a grandfather clock with an alarm louder than a police siren to his back or, better yet, a sledge hammer that rings his bell, Carla thinks as she feels herself losing control.

As Jim grabs the frying pan out of the cabinet, he steams to himself, *Why can't I just once come home to a hot cooked meal? She is always off running around with her friends while I work a long tiring day. She has probably gone shopping again and spent three times more than I made. Can't she think of anyone but herself at least once in her life?*

Have you ever had similar thoughts pull at your

temper strings? Have you wanted to re-check the marriage certificate to see what you signed up for, because you're sure it wasn't this? If so, you are normal. But there are a few things you can do to help yourself stay in control, and it starts with your thoughts.

Are your thoughts important?

How important is a thought? Very! Our thoughts turn into our beliefs, which produce our feelings, which create our words and actions. Since beliefs, feelings, words, and actions are a great part of who we are, I would say a thought is very important. Solomon said, "For as he thinks in his heart, so is he…" (Proverbs 23:7, NKJV). God's Word proves He didn't leave us clueless to the importance of a thought; it becomes whom we are. I think it is wonderful that God has given each and every one of us the ability to think about what we are thinking about. Right this minute you can stop what you are doing and think about your last thought. You can choose to continue that thought or change your thought to something else.

Supporting Scripture: Proverbs 13:16 and 1 Peter 1:13.

Another one of my most life-changing events was realizing I could decide to continue a thought or not. I have to add, it was freeing for Del also, because I began to pick my battles. I think it helped us both. I no longer felt like I could explode at any second, and he didn't have to listen to me complain about every little thing. Now I know I can make my mind, mind me. You can decide whether a thought should continue or not. Realize how important that choice is, because it affects your future and the future of others in your life.

We have to be very careful of our "me factor," which consumes our subconscious. I like to explain it as a predominate *me gene* that will try to take over every thought if we don't control it. Also known as pride, ego, selfishness, and being self-centered. I believe this me factor can be a part of what the Bible calls our sinful nature and works of the flesh. Read the following Scriptures to better understand this nature we need to be in control of.

Supporting Scripture: Romans 8:4–17, Galatians 5:19–23, and 1 Corinthians 3:3.

Opposite of our sinful nature the Holy Spirit produces love, joy, peace, patience, kindness, goodness, faithfulness, gentleness, and self-control.

Supporting Scripture: Galatians 5:22–23

Pay attention to your body.

Your first clue to stop and think about what you are thinking about is when you notice you have that uneasy feeling inside. You are upset, your heart is racing, your palms sweating, and you have tension in your shoulders, or you plainly notice you have lost your peace. Whenever you notice you have that uneasy feeling, stop yourself and think, *What was I just thinking about?*

Whenever you notice that feeling, make a decision whether that thought can continue or not. Examine and test the thought to make sure it has passed the *Bible-tested and Jesus-approved method of thinking.*

This means it needs to be in line with what the Word of God says, and it must meet the very nature of Jesus. Then and only then, let your thought continue and grow. If it doesn't pass the test, then replace your thought with what is in line with the Word of God. For example, God's Word says:

> Finally, brethren, whatever things are *true*, whatever things are *noble*, whatever things are *just*, whatever things are *pure*, whatever things are *lovely*, whatever things are of *good report*, if there is any *virtue* and if there is anything *praiseworthy*—meditate on these things. The things which you learned and received and heard and saw in me, these do, and the God of peace will be with you.
>
> Philippians 4:8–9 (NKJV)

This Scripture covers a lot of wrong thinking, along with many other Scriptures that could be used to discipline one's thought. The Bible also says, "Your attitude should be the same that Christ Jesus had" (Philippians 2:5, NLT). It is also very helpful to check your thoughts to make sure Jesus would approve them. The *Bible-tested and Jesus-approved method of thinking* should not be confused with salvation. This method is meant to encourage you to meditate on Godly ideas to create Godly peace.

> Peace I leave with you, My peace I give to you; not as the world gives do I give to you. Let not your heart be troubled, neither let it be afraid.
>
> John 14:27 (NKJV)

> These things I have spoken to you, that in Me you may have peace. In the world you will have tribulation; but be of good cheer, I have overcome the world.
>
> John 16:33 (NKJV)

Here are a few examples of scripture for *Bible-Tested and Jesus-Approved Thinking*.

You feel others are against you. - Luke 6:27–28

You are worrying about things. - Philippians 4:6–7

You are not sure what to do. - Proverbs 3:5–6

You are worrying about sin. - Romans 10:9–13 and
Psalm 103:12

You feel alone. - Romans 8:38–39

Not that by doing the method earns you salvation, because Scripture also says:

Knowing that a man is not justified by the works of the law but by faith in Jesus Christ, even we have believed in Christ Jesus, that we might be justified by faith in Christ and not by the works of the law; for by the works of the law no flesh shall be justified.

Galatians 2:16 (NKJV)

45

Make your yes be yes, and your no be no.

As Robert noticed the tall young blonde walking by, he thought, *Maybe she'll dance with me. I could bump into her and then ask her to dance. What would it hurt if I just danced one song and talked to her for a little while? Judy would never know. I only want to have a little fun and excitement. All my friends are doing it and getting by with it; one little dance can't hurt a thing.*

He smiled when he walked toward her, deceiving himself with his thoughts of lust. You have got to be kidding me, Robert! You'll be dancing, all right, and right out the door Judy slams in your face. You would not believe how many men and women are deceived by this kind of thinking. The *Bible-tested and Jesus-approved method of thinking* takes away the wishy-washy feelings you have about your thoughts and decisions. Using it will make your yeses mean yes and your no's mean no, without wasting a lot a time and energy. In other words, you have made a decision to use the Word of God as your decision maker, so you just do it, leaving the reasoning out. However, in order for this method to work, you do need to be reading the Bible. I have tried to read at least one chapter almost every day for many years, which has resulted in reading the Bible through many times. So often in my counseling I hear things like, "I believe God wants this…" However, we can't really know what He wants without knowing what His Word says.

> All Scripture is inspired by God and is useful to teach us what is true and to make us realize what is wrong in our lives. It straightens us out and teaches us to do what is right. It is God's way of preparing us in every way, fully equipped for every good thing God wants us to do.
>
> 2 Timothy 3:16–17 (NLT)

> For the word of God is full of living power. It is sharper than the sharpest knife, cutting deep into our innermost thoughts and desires. It exposes us for what we really are.
>
> Hebrews 4:12 (NLT)

If you have a special concern on your mind, you can easily go to the concordance in the back of your Bible (if your Bible has one) and look up words that pertain to your thought or problem. This will help you see firsthand what the Bible says about that subject. Books that help you find certain subjects in the Bible are also available for purchase. If you are unable to research a specific thought at a specific moment, simply use the Bible reference mentioned above and do or think whatever is true, noble, just, pure, lovely, of good report, virtue, or praiseworthy. This verse should be memorized or written down so you have access to it easily. If your thoughts don't pass the above test, stop yourself and start your thought process over.

However, in God's Word it does say that he has written his law on our hearts. What better way then to bring this law to our conscious minds by reading what his Word say about it. It will help us by taking our reasoning and sinful nature out of our final decision with a sound *Bible-tested and Jesus-approved* thinking approach to everyday thoughts. Always remember: sin is deceiving, and God's Word helps us clarify sin.

Stopping wrong thinking stops wrong words and actions.

If you follow the above advice, you could soon notice a huge difference in your relationships and life. Don't try to reason or understand everything. Trust that God made all things and knows how to handle every situation. You'll be happy to know that in my experiences—and if you follow the above advice, soon yours—God's way is the best way. It may not always be the easiest way because we have to fight our habits and character. Keep in mind we are all human, therefore we are never able to follow it perfectly. We are given the gift of the Spirit by faith, and I have definitely had the best outcomes doing things his way with his help produced in the fruits of the Spirit. "But the fruit of the Spirit is love, joy, peace, longsuffering, kindness, goodness, faithfulness, gentleness, self-control. Against such there is no law" (Galatians 5:22–23, NKJV).

Don't reason something wrong into something right.

If you are anyone like me—and you probably are because you are human—don't try to reason something that is wrong into something that is right. Sometimes when Del and I are arguing, I don't like to talk to him. I would prefer to go to another room and sit and think about how right I am and about the reasons he is wrong. Okay, I will admit, I like to stew for a little while. Believe it or not, I have stewed so long that I have had a batch made up that could have ended world hunger. There have been a few times I've known I was wrong right from the beginning, but admitting it would have been harder than throwing away my favorite pair of shoes. If I thought about it hard and long enough, I could even find reasons why maybe I had a reason to be mad. That does not help anything. As a matter of fact, it can change you and the situation for the worse.

Be honest with yourself. You can't change a bad behavior unless you know it as your own. This is the hard part; before you can change, you need to realize you need to. You don't have to feel right to make yourself do the right thing. Remember, your feelings follow your thoughts. You can't get a better outcome doing the same *wrong* thing over and over again. Are you the one common denominator to all your problems? If you don't like the results of your behavior over and over again, own it and then change it! Don't feel bad about needing to change. Feel good about knowing you need to change. Each and every one of us is responsible for the words and behavior we have that causes a response in someone else. It can be as simple as, if you don't want an explosion, don't light a match. Even the smallest changes can make the biggest differences. This is not about pointing out each other's bad behavior so don't start pointing fingers. This is about self-awareness and thinking about the thoughts you had before and after your behavior. So the next time you are mad, put yourself to the thought test, because it's good for you and your relationship!

Be motivated to think right thoughts.

It is hard to always think and act the correct way. As an example, if you had a small computer screen mounted on your forehead that broadcast to the world what you were thinking, would you be more motivated to think about what you think about? Although you don't have a computer mounted to your head, your thoughts are exposed through the words you say and the things you do. So really, in a round about way, you are exposed. If all you think about is another woman or man rather than your wife or husband, don't you think that will show up in your actions? Of course it will! If you allow that thought to continue, it could have devastating effects on your marriage and family. Make it a habit to only allow yourself to think about things that will profit you and your family. Let's look at words said like, "I don't feel in love with my husband or wife anymore." Since we know a feeling follows a thought, what have you been thinking about your partner? Obviously, if you are having these thoughts, you are not thinking about your partner in the same loving way you thought about her when you decided to marry her.

You must make yourself mix thoughts of bad behavior with thoughts of good behavior. It is very important to stop bad thoughts at their onset. As soon as you notice an uneasy feeling (and you know what feeling that is for you), *stop yourself.* Think with the fear that all your thoughts could be the headline news in tomorrow's paper, because if you choose to continue them, they could be.

Using Self-Control to Control Thoughts

A wandering mind is like a television that has been left on with no one paying any real attention to it. The shows air one after the other; you're not really choosing to watch them or not to watch them. The good or bad words go into your ears and penetrate your brain and move into your subconscious. However, if you would pay attention to the TV programs that are playing, you could stop what is going into your subconscious mind that could affect your unconscious decisions later. If you don't like that show, you can use the remote control and change the channel. Your mind is the same way when you are paying attention to it and not allowing just any thought to enter. Like a remote control can change the TV channel, you can use your self-control to change your mind or thoughts at any time. If it is not in line with what the Word of God says, or the nature of Jesus, then don't question it, just change it! A good example is when Jesus was tested in the wilderness. He did not let the lies of Satan lead him to destruction. Even though the words of Satan were confusingly close to Scripture, Jesus knew God's Word and refused to be tricked. Study Scripture and see it play out with more good thoughts, resulting in more good choices played out in the time God has ordained for you here on earth.

> And do not be conformed to this world, but be transformed by the renewing of your mind, that you may prove what is that good and acceptable and perfect will of God."
>
> Romans 12:2 (NKJV)

Filter your thoughts.

A vacuum cleaner filter is another good example of how your thoughts need to be filtered. If you were to vacuum a large mess of spilled dirt without the filter in your vacuum cleaner, you would end up with a bigger mess than you started with. The dirt would be picked up off the floor, run through your vacuum, and blown back out, depositing dirt over your entire room. Can you picture the mess? Our thoughts need to be filtered also. We can't always control the junk and dirt that we hear and see, but we can filter it in our minds through the *Bible-tested and Jesus-approved method of thinking*. If we don't filter our thoughts, we can and do end up with huge messes in our lives. But if we filter our thoughts like the vacuum cleaner filter collects dirt, we have an opportunity to clean up any messy thoughts we have before they have a chance to cause problems in our lives.

What do you want to happen?

No one ever intends on their marriage failing. We all get married with the best intentions of having a loving relationship that will last a lifetime. Almost anyone who has gone through a divorce will tell you it was the last thing they thought could happen on the day they wed. Life can get in the way, and then all of a sudden you are there. Godly people end up divorced; our sinful human nature causes us all to fall short in some way, which is why Jesus died for us. Thank you, Jesus!

It is important to decide what you want to happen in your marriage and then make clear choices at how you will get there. I call this the *Kissing and Cooking Marriage plan*. If you desire to grow old together and help each other in your old age, then you need to think now what actions it requires to accomplish it. I think there is nothing more special than to see an aged couple that has been married for years dote on each other. The other day I saw this little old man get out of the car and struggle over to his wife's side to help her out of the car and get her safely started with her cane. These love acts have to be what God had in mind when he gave Adam a helper. Acts of kindness don't have to be reserved for when you are older. Picture yourself growing old with your spouse and taking care of each other's needs with love and concern, starting now!

It is hard for me to imagine my later years alone. If God is willing, I would like Del's cute little cheeks there with me. Decide now what thoughts and behaviors it will take for your marriage to fulfill the words, "Until death do us part." What kind of a commitment to your thought-control and spouse will you have to make your marriage last?

Make a choice to think good thoughts.

Tammy's husband's voice becomes louder and louder as he tries to prove his point. He moves closer to her to make sure she understands his every profound word. Tammy suddenly notices fear climbing up her back like a loaded dump truck climbing a steep hill. The heaviness loads her with such anguish she can hardly breathe. Her heart begins to pound; she feels like it is going to explode right out of her chest. Her arms begin to come up in front of her face to protect her from a sudden blast of his temper. Jacob notices her fear, and with loving concern he gently holds her as he lowers his voice, remembering she had a boyfriend that abused her.

We all have pasts that involve others. Be sure not to transfer your hurts from others onto your spouse. If you know this is an issue for you, test yourself often. Don't make assumptions that your partner is like someone in your past. Prayerfully and/or with a professional work on correcting any faulty belief from past experiences that do not involve your spouse. If your spouse has issues from her past, be very sensitive to her needs to recover. Live in this moment, and live moment by moment. Don't waist your life thinking about who hurt you, who did what to you, or even why things happened in the first place.

Has your spouse ever done something that made you so mad that it was all you thought about all day long? Your mind went over and over it, detail by detail. You keep thinking something like, *He or she never wants to do anything with me.* Then before you knew it, you were all worked up, and it seemed to be a huge problem. Never being there is a big assumption; was it really *never?*

Only let the truth progress in your mind. This has happened to me before. When I have gotten my feelings hurt, I would think about the problem so much that soon I would forget any good Del had ever done. For example, Del likes to hunt, or should we just call him the great white hunter who doesn't know when to stop and give his wife some love. For years I would mope around and get fired-up mad at him because he wasn't spending enough of his free time with me. (I had to correct myself just now, because I was about to write "any" instead of "enough"!) The truth was, he did spend time with me, it just wasn't as much as I would have liked. Sometimes I would really get myself worked up about things like this. It made for an unhappy him and me. When I started thinking about the good things he had been doing for me, like taking our son with him hunting, cuddling as we watched TV, taking me out for dinner occasionally, and going to the lake with me during the summer, it didn't seem so bad.

Look at your partner as a whole person. Do not let yourself just concentrate on the thing your partner did that upset you. Make yourself place the bad things along with all the good things he or she has done to create a true picture of your spouse in your mind. You can't have a healthy relationship thinking about the bad he does without also thinking about the good he does. Give the bad only the amount of your thoughts it deserves. (However, physical and verbal abuse should always be taken to a professionally trained individual.) It is helpful in the times you are feeling angry to have happy memories to mix in. It is important to have these memories stored in your mind before an event like this happens. It is hard to want to find good thoughts when you are hurt and upset. List three of your partner's good qualities that you can place in your memory to pull out for times like these.

1. _____
2. _____
3. _____

The next time you find yourself upset with your partner about something she's done, make yourself mix these good qualities into your bad thoughts. You will find this makes it much easier on you to keep things in perspective. *Kissing and Cooking for Couples* will give you an opportunity to create many happy thoughts and memories of love and kindness with your partner. Store these up and pull them out of your memory bank whenever you find yourself thinking only bad thoughts of your spouse.

Do you do what you think you do?

Kent slammed the door of his car with disgust as he juggled another day of business appointments and running the kids to events. *I am the only one that does anything around this place*, he thought. *If it gets done, I have to do it. Barb never does her part. I am the one that is always caring for their needs. I get them ready for school, do their laundry, and cook their meals. I pamper Barb's every need. All I do is pamper, pamper, and pamper some more!*

Who do you see yourself to be? Are you loving, caring, rough, cold, compassionate? Think of a few words that you feel describe yourself.

_____

_____

_____

Now, for the next week, keep those words close in thought. As you go about the week, check yourself to see if you act the way you think you act and do the things you think you do. If you feel you are caring, do you do the things a caring person should do all the time or only when you feel like it? Are you caring to all people or only some people? Take an inventory and see if you see any flaws in how you really act compared to how you think you act. If you find some errors in your character, challenge yourself to become the person you think you are or want to be. Take some time to examine the space you take up in this world and how you are truly affecting it.

Thoughts are definitely important.

Without question our thoughts affect not only ourselves but also the people around us. Protect your thoughts like they are a precious gift. When they are controlled and paid attention to, they will not only be a precious gift of peace for you but also for the ones God has given you to share your life with.

Good thoughts create good words, which create good actions, which create peace in your marriage.

We Ordered Caviar, Where is the Caviar?

Terry was Becky's dream come true. She thought she would never find Mr. Right. Low and behold her eyes turned dreamy the first moment she saw him. He was her "knight in shining armor" the day he was sent from the plumbing company to fix her plugged drain wearing coveralls and a tool belt. She would girlishly melt every time she saw him for months after their first encounter. But something had changed. Now she dreaded him coming home with dirty clothes and boots, expecting supper waiting at the table. It was all she could do to hold back her unhappy thoughts and wonder how she had become the wife of this man?

The Honeymoon Feeling

"The Honeymoon feeling is gone! What do I do?"

Many frustrated and disappointed spouses say those words. Is your marriage everything you hoped and dreamed it would be? Did you think you ordered caviar and now feel like you're being served snapping turtle? If I could tell a newly-married couple only one thing that would benefit them to know before their marriage, it would be without a doubt: to expect their marriage to be different than they planned and thought it would be. Expectations can ruin the hopes and dreams of what is really just a normal stage in a healthy relationship.

If you knew you would be hurt and irritated throughout your marriage by the person you love, would you marry him anyway? We all have a few behaviors that can drive our loved ones nuts. The first stage of love can cover up some of our irritating habits.

"Isn't her talkative nature cute? She loves to talk about all my favorite things."

"He is the life of the party. I have so much fun with him."

Soon, when the honeymoon is over, those things you thought were so heavenly start tugging on your nerves.

"Will she ever quit talking, so I can watch my favorite sport?"

"Will he ever grow up and act like a man?"

If you have similar thoughts ringing through your head, *you are normal and in a normal relationship!*

What is love?

What is real love? Love is understanding and accepting the person you love even though you know she's not perfect. Love is picking up the dirty clothes you just tripped over. Love is eating a special meal that you can hardly choke down. Love is an unending dose of happiness and unhappiness.

In Galatians it says love is the fruit of the spirit. "But the fruit of the Spirit is love, joy, peace, longsuffering, kindness, goodness, faithfulness, gentleness, self-control" (Galatians 5:22–23, NKJV). Unfortunately, there is not a perfect person out there. So know you are not alone. We are all in the same boat going down the same river of frustration. The Bible tells us that Jesus was the only human being who lived a perfect life. It also says in the book of Romans that no one else will ever follow in His footsteps of perfection. "for all have sinned and fall short of the glory of God, being justified freely by His grace through the redemption that is in Christ Jesus" (Romans 3:23–24, NKJV). It doesn't say "some" fall short; it says "all" fall short. Know you will have to forgive your partner and be disappointed from time to time.

Realize the world is not what it seems to be.

We can appear like we are the best and happiest person who ever lived when the truth is, we just had a huge fight that could have awoken a coma patient. It's funny how we must think our spouses go deaf when we are trying to prove a point to them. It's like we think it will penetrate further into their brains and hit a soft spot if we yell. This is not true—it only fuels their temper.

Your friends,' co-workers,' and relatives' relationships are not always what they appear to be. We are all at times embarrassed to reveal our bad behavior or the bad behavior of our loved one. I think the world would be much better if we would share our shortcomings with one another. If we were to reveal our true natures, others would not be misled into thinking their lives are so bad. Our expectations for others and ourselves would be more realistic. But in saying all this, it does not relieve us from working on our weaknesses and building on our strengths in our relationships. Maybe being more exposed would even make us try harder to be better people. Maybe revealing our weaknesses could help us conquer our shortcoming more effectively and become a better society as a whole. This has always been very hard for me to do. I think I've been afraid people would not like me as much if they knew all the stupid things I've done. Some things I can't even believe I've done myself. Scripture says we are to confess our sins to one another, or better known as supporting one another in our weaknesses. Be the best friend, partner, and relative you can be.

It's not always fifty/fifty.

I heard a preacher explain love in a marriage this way. You will not always feel in love. As a matter of fact, there will be times you will question whether you like your partner at all. It isn't a question of if you will fall out of love with your partner from time to time. It is a prayer that you never fall out of love at the same time. Your marriage will not always be a fifty/fifty relationship. At times your love and commitment will need to be eighty percent when your spouse is only at twenty percent. At times yours will only be thirty percent while your spouse's will need to increase to seventy percent. Marriage is all about give and take and the realization that you will be giving and taking the rest of your life. It may feel like a tug of war at times, but it is really giving and sacrificing when your spouse is weak and him returning the favor during your tough times.

What is not realistic in a relationship?

Because there will be good and bad times in your relationship, there may be times you will need to seek counseling. If you notice behaviors such as verbal and physical abuse, adultery, or extreme unresolved conflict and other questionable behaviors, you need to ask for help. This doesn't mean your marriage is hopeless; it just means that you need someone to guide and help you make good choices. If you are ever questioning a marital behavior, don't hesitate to contact a professional and seek their guidance. There may be times in your marriage when you will need the help of a third party to see a new way to approach an unresolved problem. Too often couples don't seek counseling until it is so bad that their marriage is only hanging by a thread. I can't stress enough, as soon as you notice unresolved problems, contact professional help before your marriage seems beyond repair.

Let's Spend the Night Together—Kissing!

When Kathy and Bill first started dating, they could spend hours and hours sitting on the porch swing talking about nothing. They listened to each other's every word. Three children later she can't get him to spend one evening a week with her. Bill started his dream business and everything is going well. He is providing very well for all the monetary needs of his family. Kathy takes her evening bath, finding herself feeling alone and desiring the touch and love of her husband. Bill stays late at the office once again, unaware of his wife's yearning desires.

Are you nourishing your marriage?

Do you spend even a quarter of the time alone with your spouse as you did when you were dating? Why?

Couples just live; they don't plan to have a successful, happy, fulfilling, loving relationship. We are a busy generation. We are busy with work, busy with the kids, busy with the house, busy with friends, busy with hobbies, or we simply pay more attention to the television than our spouse. We are entirely too busy being busy or distracted by less important things.

What time does this leave you for nourishing your marriage? If you are like most couples, not much. We are guilt-ridden to spend time with our children because we are working parents. The best thing you can do for your children is to spend time keeping a healthy relationship with your spouse. We don't have to look very hard to see the effect divorce has on children. Tag-team weekends and holidays, listening to one parent bad-mouth the other, and many tug-of-war feelings delivered from unaware and loving parents. Don't sacrifice your relationship now for your kids, because if you do, your kids could suffer later. Make a commitment to put the needs of your relationship before *unnecessary* needs of your children. Do it knowing it is the best thing for your kids, even more so than taking them to one more activity.

A marriage is a special bond between two loving people. However, it doesn't stay that way on its own. Just like anything else you do, your marriage is only going to be what you make it. We can see this in friendships. A person who was once a best friend becomes a past acquaintance if you don't stay in touch. The same will happen in your loving marriage if you don't protect and cherish it every day. Knowing the number of marriages that have failed should show us we need to pay attention to our own most valuable person. It is a real problem. You can't just take your marriage for granted anymore. Divorce happens to good people who never thought it would happen to them. Studies have shown that about sixty percent of divorced couples wished they had worked harder to keep their marriage. We can't continue to sit around thinking it will never happen to us. We can realize marriage is tough, and we have a responsibility to do everything we can to protect it and plan for its success.

Plan special times together.

It is advised time and time again to plan a date night with your spouse, but how many of us do it? Just like anything else, we feel that is for someone else. Time alone is so important. That is when we find out how things are going in each other's lives. It gives us an opportunity to really listen, to know what is important to each other. I can't stress enough how important it is to spend time with each other. Don't feel like you are sacrificing anything to do it, because you are really sacrificing everything if you don't do it.

Be each other's new hobby. When you have a hobby, you buy what you need to do it. You set aside time to enjoy it, and you find out all there is to know about it. Within your personal hobby (your spouse), you should find something that you both like to do. Walking, biking, boating, going to dinner, *Kissing and Cooking*, giving back rubs, or just simply spend the night kissing. It doesn't matter what you do together, just so you take time to do it.

Is there a secret to a happy marriage?

The secret of a happy marriage is really not a secret at all; the secret is simply to keep the romance alive. Anything living needs to be fed, and so does your relationship. Start thinking of romance as a day-to-day event and not always a special occasion. Do small little kindnesses for each other. Put a note in his or her briefcase, lunch pail, or laundry basket. Tell her you love her at an unexpected time. Have a glass of wine or lemonade waiting for him when he gets home from a hard day of work. Use your creative juices and think of something that doesn't take a lot of effort but will let her know she is loved.

Respect each other's interests.

Spend time together respecting each other's interests, even when you really don't enjoy doing what your spouse loves to do. Think of it this way; instead of loving what he loves, love watching him enjoy what he loves.

I have had a lot of practice in my marriage doing this. My husband is into racing. Shortly after we were married, he bought a go-cart, followed by a mini-sprint. Then, when my son was old enough to fit into a go-cart, my son started racing and is now in a modified racecar. My love was not racing, and there were many other things I would rather be doing. However, I went along with it because I enjoyed seeing my husband doing what he had always wanted to do.

On the other hand, my love is the lake. I feel I could spend my whole life there. Well, not so for my husband. He has gone along with it because he knows I love it. I'm not sure if he would say because he loves seeing me happy. I think it is more because he hates seeing me mad!

It is important to spend time together doing what makes each of you happy. This is definitely one of those things that will need to be approached with a big dose of give and take. I'll go racing with you, honey, if you go to the lake with me! We both win. I don't really mind going to the races with him, and

I don't think he really minds going to the lake with me.

Have some interests of your own also.

After saying how important it is to spend time together, it is important to have your own interests also. We can't be attached at the hip all the time. I do feel it is important to have your own time within reason, with one exception. I don't feel you can have a healthy relationship going out on the town without each other. I have seen girls' or boys' night out ruin many marriages. This is the one thing I feel very strongly about. I have heard couples say they can't afford a babysitter to justify going out together. Let me tell you, you can't *not* afford one. You may never mean to or think you will notice someone of the opposite sex, but it happens. It can be easily avoided by going out together and flirting with your own special date! This is something Del and I decided early in our marriage. We both liked to go out, and right away we noticed the problems it can cause when couples don't do things together. This was one of those adjustments you make when you can see problems ahead. I would say if I would have to choose one of the most important decisions we made together about our marriage, this would have to be one of them.

What you put time into can become great.

When you put time into your lawn, it looks great. When you put time into your car, it runs great. When time is put into a meal, it tastes great. What I'm saying is that anything that has good results takes time and loving care. Don't spend all your time doing things that don't really matter. It would be like stuffing yourself with cold meat sandwiches until you are miserable and then realize you could have had a large piece of chocolate cream pie if you would have eaten one less sandwich. You could have enjoyed the good stuff also!

The time you put into your marriage can become a lifetime of happy memories for you and your children. So don't use up all your time on things that don't really matter and not leave enough time for the things that do—like the person you chose to spend your life with.

Time creates memories, memories create feelings, and feelings create love.

Isn't Kissing Communicating?

Jack quietly leaned over to give Lois a kiss before he left for work. She felt the light touch on her cheek and rolled over to a deep sleep. An hour later she awoke and hurried the kids to school. She drove herself home, wishing she had someone to talk to. She longed for one of their heartfelt talks like they used to share. Their lives are so full of work, kids, events, and chores that they had not noticed the only communicating they had been experiencing for a while was their morning kiss.

Communication, communication, communication!

Communication is to relationships what "Location, location, location!" is to property. It can make or break the deal. Good communication in a relationship is a must, and it is something that cannot be taken lightly. It doesn't really matter how many differences you have; what matters is if you know how to communicate those differences in a non-confrontational, loving way. In survey after survey, the number one problem couples list in their marriage is the lack of communication and the skills required to have an understanding relationship. They don't understand each other and don't know how to resolve their differences in a Godly way.

It would be impossible to talk about communication without making a clear link to the fact that we are all made different. Keep in mind the information that was discussed in the section, "Know your differences." Don't focus on your differences, but embrace what you each have to offer for each situation. Always remember there can be two ways to get to the same result. In love, does it really matter how you get there?

What is communication?

Is it listening, or is it talking? Communication is so much more than these two things. Communication is really sharing your thoughts and feelings through spoken and written words, actions, signs, emotion, and more. Sharing is the key word here. We teach our children to share and feel we are teaching them a good behavior. Sharing is a "kindness" word. It is about the owner of something (in the case of communication, a thought) giving it away to someone else. Sharing in a marriage is really giving or receiving information for the *profit* of another person. Communication involves more than just hearing or seeing—it also requires interpreting the information in its intended way. It's about communicating through words, actions, and tones so the listener will understand you the way you intended them to understand you.

The other day I realized I misunderstood what someone was saying. I asked a man how his wife was doing. He said she was doing fine; that she had started a new job working three nights a week, stocking shelves in a local store after business hours. He went on to say how nice it was that she had that job. I perceived him to be saying that his wife really liked working when there was no one around to bug her and enjoyed working only three days a week. But after listening to him a little longer, I realized he meant it was nice for him to have the house to himself three nights a week! Realizing this, I gave him a sideways smile, and then he added, with a smile, "I am just joking around, of course."

It is very important for you to communicate in a way that your meaning can be easily understood without the possibility of another interpretation. If you find yourself in a situation that you're unsure if your spouse has interpreted your words correctly, ask her what she heard you say. If you're not sure you interpreted him correctly, repeat back to him what you heard, then ask if it was correct.

More is being said than what comes out of your mouth.

Gestures, tone, posture, body, and facial movements can often convey what you don't say when you are talking. Some people can be especially sensitive to this. So pay close attention to your non-verbal actions, such as pointing fingers, stomping feet, making faces, and turning your back.

Sometimes Del doesn't have to say a word for me to think I know what he is saying. Especially that rolling of the eyes movement—it seems clear to me that whatever I just said, he thought it was stupid. His unspoken communication causes me to make an interpretation of his unspoken communication. Of course, he never meant it like *that*. I must admit, at times this may make me think about what I said or did. It can bring bad behavior to my attention or make me realize he didn't agree with what I just said. Either way, I think it would be better for him to verbalize what he meant rather than making a confrontational gesture. Verbalizing your thoughts allows less room to be misunderstood.

Strengthen your communication.

Kissing and Cooking for Couples can be one of your most valuable tools to strengthen the communication in your relationship. While preparing each recipe, you will be asked to answer prepared questions to initiate intimate communication. These questions are triggered to get you outside of your normal conversations and create an emotional bond that will strengthen your marriage. The questions are to be approached in a positive way to stimulate deep-down-in-your-soul conversations that will encourage an everlasting bond with your soul mate.

Del and I have always communicated daily—but not in the intimate way provided through this book. This has given us an opportunity to share feelings we would not normally share in our normal conversations. I feel the only way you can communicate in a way to get this kind of intimate response is to keep the following in mind:

Love like you're not afraid of being *hurt!*
Give like you're not afraid of being *taken for granted!*
Share like you're not afraid of being *exposed!*
Love like you're not afraid of being *rejected*.

This also teaches you how to respond to your partner.

It is necessary to not just read the above phrases. I would like you to truly feel the meaning of each phrase. What feelings (thoughts) would you have to change to allow yourself to let your deepest feelings (thoughts) out? Do you feel you can expose your deepest feelings in a place of safety within your relationship? Can you open up to each other in a way of pure humility? Will you respond with love to the pure humility presented to you?

Let your partner inside so he or she can experience the way you feel deep down. Admittedly your partner may not have the same feelings but will have an opportunity to truly understand you in a way he or she has never understood you before. The unsaid rule regarding this whole-hearted communication is: at no time can the information be used to trick or guilt your loved-one into something, and it must never be told to another living soul without your spouse's permission. This unspoken rule is better known as *trust!* Depending on your relationship, some of you may need to start this with baby steps.

Who do you dream to be?

We all know the person we dream to be. Now think about the person you are now. A dream or hope is something that is deep down inside all of us. We know the person we are right now and also have hope for the person we someday want to be. Remember that you are sharing your life with a person who also has a dream of the person he wants to be, yet he is forced to look in the mirror at the person he is now (realizing he has room to grow). So be very sensitive when you deal with each other on issues.

During your sharing times, I strongly encourage you to share with your partner the person you hope to become someday—no matter how "out there" you feel your dream is. These are to be deep personal dreams of who or what you want to accomplish in the days God has ordained for you while you're on earth. Let your mate experience the most intimate feelings from the person he or she has married. Sharing who you want to be lets your partner see humility in you because you are expressing your faults and unfulfilled hopes and dreams, which can give your partner a whole new respect for you. Next, allow your partner to share his or her dreams in the same way to you. Ask what you can do that would assist them in making the dreams come to reality. It is impossible for someone to help make your dreams come true if you don't tell them what they are. Your mate cannot read your mind and should not be expected to always "just know" if you haven't told him or her! Don't just give hints to what you want and become mad when they don't respond to your hint. Let them know what you would like out of them and then let them express if they are able to respond to your needs.

Communicate straight from the heart.

Communicate straight from your heart. Any other way is just words that confuse the understanding of what you truly want. Can you hold someone responsible for his or her words and actions if they don't know exactly what you really desire? Love and understanding is something you give away to your spouse (a wonderful gift), not just what you take from him for yourself. When you love for the benefit of others rather than for the benefit of you, then you will truly start to experience love the way God intended it to be. Love one another. What does that mean to you? It doesn't say to just love someone when you feel love back from that person. Simply love one another the way Jesus loves us. Remember, God loved us first.

He didn't wait until we were without sin to send His Son to save us. We shouldn't wait until our spouse is perfect to love her either. Admittedly this is easier said than done. In fact, it will never be done by any of us perfectly in this lifetime because of our human nature to sin and the *me factor* discussed earlier!

What are your spouse's emotional needs?

The book *The Five Love Languages* by Gary Chapman describes how to express heartfelt commitment to your mate. The book shows that love can be expressed in five different ways: words of affirmation, quality time, receiving gifts, acts of service, and physical touch. This book is a great informational tool in every marriage. *Kissing and Cooking* is an avenue to express all of the languages described in his book.

The Book	*Kissing and Cooking*
Words of affirmation	Topics and questions.
Quality time	It is the two of you alone.
Receiving gifts	Exchanging cards.
Acts of service	Cooking food for each other.
Physical touch	Kissing!

Get yourself a copy of the book and find out which one of the five love languages your spouse responds to best. Then use it to make his life with you the best it can be by responding in love to his needs in a way he understands.

Your Attitudes Matters

If your spouse feels important to you, it will give her a feeling of importance. When you trust him, it will make him feel trustworthy. When we realize someone has high expectations of us, we want to do our best to live up to the expectations. If someone encourages and believes in us, it makes us feel we can do it. We all like people who like us. Encouragement and respect are very important in any relationship. Whether it's a parent-child, business, friendship, or marriage relationship, it can soften any situation.

When I started to work on this book, Del was very encouraging and shared with me the benefit he thought this might have on marriages. During the process it has taken a lot to stay focused and committed to this project. Hearing a few encouraging words at the beginning from someone I love and respect has given me the boost of confidence to stay determined to finish. His belief in me has made me believe in myself. Yet I can't get my value from someone else's opinion of me, God is my true strength, as stated so many times in the Bible. Share (give away something to benefit others) kind words with the people who mean the most to you, or just anyone in general. You have nothing to lose—but everything to gain—from their response.

Do you tell others what to do or ask for their help?

We don't tell our loved ones what to do. We ask to have our requests fulfilled from each other because we love and care about each other's feelings and wants. Depending on how you look at a request can make all the difference. When you ask for something, are you asking for help, or are you demanding obedience? When you respond, are you obeying a command, or are you fulfilling a loved one's need? How you look at this will determine your attitude.

Del has always told me that I don't like being told what to do. Really I think that is true for just about everyone. However, if I look at it as if I am being asked to fulfill his needs and be his helper, that totally changes my attitude.

I think it also helps a great deal to ask for something in a polite way. If you are asked politely, the request naturally doesn't seem so demanding. Rather it makes you feel like you are fulfilling a request to meet someone's desire.

"Honey, would you please grab me a glass of water? I'm thirsty," is much better than, "Get me a glass of water." "Would you please" *always* sounds better than "Get!"

Love cannot be demanded from your spouse. It is a free gift given away by the owner, and it is a lot easier to give when there is a feeling of respect coming from your spouse. After a request is fulfilled, always make sure your spouse understands how much you appreciate what he or she did for you with a "Thank you." It will make it much easier to respond to a request in love the next time you are asked.

Practice good communication skills.

Effective communication allows your spouse to understand what you are saying and feel what you are feeling without the threat of being judged. It makes it okay in a relationship for her to be the person God made her.

Good communication skills are important not only in a marriage relationship but in any business, family, or friend relationship you may have in your life. A good rule of thumb is to care more about your relationship than your own opinion. Keep peace rather than causing conflict by realizing everyone is entitled to his or her own opinion. Don't be closed-minded by feeling that everyone is only entitled to your opinion. In every confrontation with people, check yourself to this rule: Am I forcing *my* opinion on them or giving them the freedom to their *own* opinion?

In your marriage:
Ask, Listen, Listen, Listen, Ask, Listen, Listen,
and Listen some more!

Cook because you need to, *listen* because you learn,
and *kiss* because you want to!

Let's Kiss and Make up!

How do you get from a conflict to a compromise? To start, keep in mind these human responses:

> Kindness creates Kindness
> Love creates Love
> Anger creates Anger
> Compromise creates Compromise.

It is important to keep in mind that when someone is being kind, it is easier to respond in kindness. When someone shows you love, it is easier to respond in love. If someone is communicating in anger, this will only fuel another's anger. If someone is trying to move toward you by compromising, it is easier to move toward that person with a compromise.

Sherrie and Patrick seemed to fight over the same things time after time. They each had different ideas of what they thought they should spend their money on. Sherrie wanted a new outfit, and Patrick wanted new golf clubs. There differences regarding money were taking a toll on their marriage. They needed a tool to help them find a compromise for situations like these.

Conflict is inevitable; compromise is a choice.

There is no doubt that in your marriage you will have conflicts or disagreements from time to time. It is impossible for two people to be knit together in such a way as in the union of marriage and not clash in their ideas or principles at times. Colossians says:

Therefore, as the elect of God, holy and beloved, put on tender mercies, kindness, humility, meekness, longsuffering bearing with one another, and forgiving one another, if anyone has a complaint against another; even as Christ forgave you so you also must do. But above all things put on love, which is the bond of perfection. And let the peace of God rule in your hearts, to which also you were called in one body; and be thankful.

Colossians 3:12–15 (NKJV)

In a nutshell, expect to have differences and expect to force yourself to work on those differences. A conflict has the ability to draw you closer together with a greater understanding of each other, or a conflict can split you like a great earthquake splits the ground you walk on, without much warning.

Resolve conflicts like a best ballgame of golf.

It is important when faced with a conflict to have a workable tool designed to help you through your issues. I would like to compare this process to a game of best ball in golf. In the golf game two people are a team, using each other's strengths (or balls) to win the game. You play off each other's best shots. The same is true in compromising. You both throw out ideas and use each other's best points to move on. When you get the ball in the hole, you both win no matter who makes the shot. When you come to a workable compromise, you both win, no matter who came up with the idea. You don't win by challenging each other; you win by working off each other's strength's. You either both win in marriage or you both lose.

Using the Tool and How to Get to a Compromise

1. *Describe issues:* Decide to play the game. Sit next to each other—not across the table—creating an environment for a teammate rather than a rival. Realize what you are doing now is not working and a change of approach is a must. Agree that you will use this model to come to a compromise. Remember this: kindness creates kindness, love creates love, anger creates anger, and compromise creates compromise. You must be in the mood to find common ground, so the atmosphere should be happy and hopeful, not hurt, sad, or angry. If you both are not feeling this way, decide together to use this method in an hour or the next day. Use the following tool to clarify issues.

Approach only one issue at a time. And remember to stay in the present. Don't add past hurts to this issue.

Each describe the problem or issues:

Her description:

_____

_____

_____

His description:

_____

_____

_____

2. *What do we agree on regarding issues in this conflict?* (For examples: we both love the kids/each other. We both want to get along. We both like to save money.) Finding agreements promotes working toward a solution together. List at least three commonalities.

_____

_____

_____

Play off what you do agree on rather than what you don't!

3. *What God-given temperament differences contribute to this conflict?* (Examples: non-confrontational/confrontational, conservative/non-conservative, worker/player, hobbies, religion, morals, etc.) Be detailed. Remember, we were all made to be different—not necessarily wrong or right, just different. It is important to understand that your personal differences create your differences as a couple. Know that it is acceptable to agree to disagree on some issues. List three differences contributing to this issue/problem.

His and her differences:

_____

_____

_____

Play off of allowing each other to be different people with different ideas.

4. *What is your real need compared to wants on the issue?* Use this time to brainstorm. It is important to determine if your requests regarding the issue are needs or wants. Be realistic about your needs. The only way you can change something bad is to be truthful to yourself about your part in the problem. Help by eliminating your *wants* to promote compromise. Each evaluate your own wants and needs with no help from each other. Be truthful and use this biblical principal: "therefore comfort each other and edify one another ..." (1 Thessalonians 5:11, NKJV).

Her needs:

_____

_____

_____

His needs:

_____

_____

_____

Her wants:

_____

_____

_____

His wants:

_____

_____

_____

Play off each other's needs.

5. *What are your feelings regarding the issue?* These should be your deep down feelings, which don't always have to make sense. Describe why you feel the way you do. Many times you can misunderstand each other's true feelings. (For examples: you say, "I don't feel you love me because you don't say it." But your partner does love you, even though he or she does not say it very often. You say, "I feel unappreciated because you never say thank you." But your partner does appreciate all you do, just didn't realize you needed to hear it.) Hear each other out—feelings are feelings. See if there is anything you can do to

help clarify these misunderstandings. Give up to five minutes of *uninterrupted* communication each. Listening will make him feel important to you. Use "I" statements rather than "you" statements. "God's Word say's, 'A gentle answer turns away wrath, but a harsh word stirs up anger' (Proverbs 15:1, NLT)."

Her feelings: I feel

_____

_____

His feelings: I feel you misunderstand.

_____

_____

His feelings: I feel

_____

_____

Her feelings: I feel you misunderstand.

_____

_____

Play off the feelings you do understand.

6. *Selfish solutions verses unselfish solutions.* It is important for each of you to own your own selfishness. What part of the problem/issue should you accept as your own? A selfish solution takes only your view and feelings into consideration. Feel open to express your selfish solutions to show yourself it is selfish and to show your partner you are compromising. An unselfish solution takes into consideration your partner's feelings and needs along with your feeling and needs. Each of you list a few selfish solutions and a few unselfish solutions in regard to the problem, with no help from your partner!

Selfish solutions:

His

_____

_____

Hers

_____

_____

Unselfish solutions:

His

_____

_____

Hers

_____

_____

Play off each other's unselfish solutions.

7. *What is the best compromise?* What will work for both of you? What will solve the issue/problem? Compromising is an agreement reached by both sides, settling a dispute by mutually giving and taking then sacrificing for each other. If you feel you have a workable idea, start the statement below without worrying about rejection. Take turns until you agree. God's Word says, "Love does not demand its own way..." *(*1 Corinthians 13:5, NLT).

Are you willing to agree on

_____

_____?

Are you willing to agree on

_____

_____?

You both win Par Seven. Continue statement above until you reach an agreement.

Throwing in the Towel

There are times after Del and I have been in an argument that I still feel we are in disagreement, yet I don't want to fight anymore. I just want us to get along! Maybe this is the time to waive the white flag? For this occasion, I have come up with a small dishtowel that says, *"Wanna Kiss?"* Waiving this towel doesn't mean we agree, but it does mean I want to get along and talk about the problem later; I want to agree to disagree for right now. This towel should be placed in with your other dishtowels so either party can easily find it. To purchase an official *"Wanna Kiss?"* towel and other relationship products, visit www.kissingandcooking.com.

If no agreement can be made, agree to discuss the issue at another time. This will allow you each to have time to think about the other's solutions. Consider discussing the issue with a professional mediator. *But do not let issues go unresolved for long periods of time!*

Things to Keep in Mind

1. Stop trying to get what you want, and start helping your spouse get what he or she wants.
2. If you are into playing games, join an adult league team, because the mind games don't belong in a relationship. Say what you want to say and be open to a discussion in regard to what you say.
3. Don't focus on your problem; focus on your solution to the problem. That means to stop concentrating on why you are mad at your partner and start trying to figure out how the situation can be changed so you are both happy.
4. Ask yourself, are you encouraging the problem or the solution?
5. We can't change others—that is God's job.

We can only change our attitude about other's behaviors and pray that God will change them.

6. Nagging can come across as being pushy and give your partner a sense of being stupid.

7. Help your spouse to feel safe in your relationship; don't attack areas of fear or weakness.

8. For better or worse was put in your vows because you need to expect the "worse" to be mixed in with the "better" throughout your marriage.

9. Be realistic in your expectations; all couples have some issues they never resolve or come to an agreement on.

10. Tackle the problem as teammates; you and I are against the problem or issue, and two minds are better than one in finding a solution.

11. The tongue is like a *hot* pepper. It has the ability to get someone fired up on the spot.

12. Control your tongue because you are responsible for the words you say that activate a response in someone else.

13. We all want trust and respect in our marriages. What behaviors and actions do you have to get it from your spouse?

14. What kind of example are you for your spouse?

Are you an example of how you want to be treated? If you were accused of being a good spouse, would there be enough evidence to convict you in a court of law?

15. Realize what affects you also affects your spouse. Make choices that are good for both of you.

16. Realize what your spouse complains or nags about are her wants, which you are not meeting; start trying to meeting these needs, or explain why you can't, and see if your relationship changes.

17. Everyone has good and bad days. We are all sharing our bad days with someone. Is there anyone in your life who is happier seeing you walk out of the room than into it? Be sunshine, not clouds.

18. Who's putting up with your bad days?

19. Who are you expecting to make you happy? If it is not God, you will surely be disappointed.

20. God's Word says, "I can do all things through Christ who strengthens me" (Philippians 4:13, NKJV). "All things" includes compromising.

21. Failure, conflict, and being wrong all provide opportunities to learn something or stretch yourself to a new level of understanding.

Love Me Tenderly

Do you focus more on how to give love to your spouse or how much love you have received from your spouse? We are all selfish by nature—some a little and some a lot, depending on our temperaments. I challenge you for just one day to see how often you focus on the needs of others rather than how everything affects your life. This can really be an eye opener for everyone. I would like to consider myself caring, but when I put myself to the test, I realized I was compassionate to others but only after I saw the effect it would have on my life. I did want to fulfill what Jesus said was the new commandment, to "... *love one another...*" (John 13:34, NKJV), but in all honesty, only after I agonized how it would affect my time, feelings, money, reputation, and so on. We will all focus on different things, depending on our own special temperament. Self-centeredness is a big obstacle for all of us to try to overcome.

Don't just pretend that you love others. Really love

them. Hate what is wrong. Stand on the side of the good. Love each other with genuine affection, and take delight in honoring each other.

Romans 12:9–10 (NLT)

What is love?

The Bible says in 1 John, "...God is love..." (1 John 4:16, NKJV). He is talking about our Creator, the God who created each and every one of us and everything we come in contact with. Everything about God is love. Isn't this hard to grasp?

God showed how much he loved us by sending his only Son into the world so that we might have eternal life through him. This is real love. It is not that we loved God, but that he loved us and sent his Son as a sacrifice to take away our sins. Dear friends, since God loved us that much, we surely ought to love each other.

1 John 4:9–11 (NLT)

Since God is love, he had to do for us what we were unable to do. In this we know one thing love is: doing for someone what he or she can't do him or herself. I have often thought how wonderful it is for me that God sent Jesus to die for my sins. My selfishness has viewed this gift as totally for me, one sided. (It's not all about me.) But when you look at the very nature of God, He is love, and God's nature needed to give this love. It is the only thing God could do because He is *love*.

> Love suffers long and is kind; love does not envy; love does not parade itself, is not puffed up; does not behave rudely, does not seek its own, is not provoked, thinks no evil; does not rejoice in iniquity, but rejoices in the truth; bears all things, believes all things, hopes all things, endures all things.
>
> 1 Corinthians (13:4–7, NKJV)

Not only does this passage explain what we should try to do, but it also explains to us what God is doing and what God has done. God made man to be in fellowship with him. After the fall of man, we have been separated from God. I have always looked at that separation concentrating on the effect it had on me, not the effect it had on God. *"God is Love."* He did not want to be separated from us, and I know I truly don't understand how much I don't want to be separated from Him. It is hard to think in this fast-paced world that it is *not all about here.* It is still truly all about being back where we should be with our Heavenly Creator. We hear these precious words in the book of John so often but without giving them much deep thought.

> For God so loved the world that He gave His only begotten Son, that whoever believes in Him should not perish but have everlasting life. For God did not send His Son into the world to condemn the world, but that the world through Him might be saved.
>
> John 3:16–17 (NKJV)

What are we saved to? *We are saved back to Him!* We will be back in his presence when we go to our heavenly home. God himself is a good example of love. Now read these words again; what is love?

Love suffers long and is kind; love does not envy;
love does not parade itself, is not puffed up; does
not behave rudely, does not seek its own, is not
provoked, thinks no evil; does not rejoice in iniquity,
but rejoices in the truth; bears all things, believes all
things, hopes all things, endures all things.

1 Corinthians 13:4–7 (NKJV)

Our God has given us a perfect example of what
love is through His Son Jesus. Not that we can ever
demonstrate this love perfectly. But God has given
us strength through Him to use our self-control to
strive toward the goal. This goal is, as Jesus said, to
"...love one another as I have loved you" (John 15: 12,
NKJV).

Considerations for Love in a Marriage

1. Share how much you need your spouse. It is a
    human want to be needed.
2. Love in a marriage is caring about someone's

well being so much you actually experience and feel their hurts when they feel upset.

3. Love is focusing on your spouse's happiness and well being more than your own.

4. Pray that God will help you over any selfishness and give you the ability to focus on the needs of the people He has placed in your life to love.

5. Love is not only a feeling you enjoy from time to time but is something you will need to choose to do when you don't feel like it and don't want to.

6. Expect perfect love to come from God, not your spouse.

Then what is love in a marriage?

The Bible says love suffers long, is kind, does not envy, does not parade itself, is not puffed up, does not behave rudely, does not seek its own, is not provoked, thinks no evil, does not rejoice in iniquity, rejoices in the truth, bears all things, believes all things, hopes all things, and endures all things. *When you read these, are you focusing more on loving or being loved?*

Final Thoughts

Love your partner God's way because you want to please God, not because your spouse deserves it. (Do it with an attitude that understands that God does not give us what we deserve because of His Son's sacrifice on the cross.)

We all desire to give and receive love as the Bible states. However, if you question certain behaviors in your relationship, seek the help of a professionally-trained person to determine if you are in a harmful situation as soon as possible.

My prayer for you is straight from the Word of God: "So I pray that God, who gives you hope, will keep you happy and full of peace as you believe in him. May you overflow with hope through the power of the Holy Spirit" (Romans 15:13, NLT).

Menu One

Almond Chicken Crescent Entree
Flavored Orange Greens
Glazed Apple Roll–Ups

Special instructions to make your date great!

1. Read recipe entirely before starting.
2. Set out all your ingredients and baking dishes.
3. If only one has time to cook, both of you do the topics and dinner instructions.
4. If one falls behind, pitch in and help him or her.
5. Put the kids to bed, or get them a movie, so you can have time alone.

Pantry Items	Produce	Other
5 T. olive oil	1 large garlic clove	2/3 C mayonnaise
½ C. sugar	1 small onion	¼ C. (or one stick)
½ t. cinnamon	1 C. chopped celery	butter
8 oz. can water	1 bunch lettuce	2 chicken breasts
chestnuts	1 orange	2-3 oz. blue cheese
Pinch of nutmeg	1 apple	4 slices Swiss cheese
1 T. vinegar		water
10.5 oz. cream of chicken		8 refrigerator crescents
¼ C. slivered almonds		
11 oz. can mandarin		
oranges		

Cut out the cards below and finish the statement and place at table to be exchanged and read during dinner.

For Her
I need you because...

For Him
I need you because...

Kissing and Cooking

Kissing and Cooking

Almond Chicken Crescent Entree

For Him: Cut 2 chicken breasts into bite-sized cubes. Heat olive oil in frying pan. Pan-fry the chicken until cooked thoroughly and golden brown. Season it as desired. Preheat oven to 375°. Go to next step while cooking, but keep an eye on the chicken! Kiss her twice while your chicken is cooking.

Preparation topic (take turns answering): What is your favorite type of kiss? Would you like to show me?

For Her: *Finely chop 1 large garlic clove. Place in large bowl. Chop one small onion. Set a small amount aside for salad, and place the rest in the bowl with the clove. If you tear up, have him kiss your tear. Tidy up if you have time.*

For Him: Dice 1 C. celery. Place in bowl with other ingredients. Check on the chicken breasts, and if done, remove from the frying pan.

For Her: *Place 1 can cream of chicken in the bowl. Sneak him his favorite kiss.*

For Him: Chop one 8 oz. can water chestnuts. Set a small amount aside for the salad and place the rest in the bowl. Place cooked chicken breast in bowl. Add 2/3 C. mayonnaise to the mixture in the bowl. Tidy up if you have time.

For Her: *Add ¼ C. water to the bowl. Mix the bowl contents together and place in sprayed 8 x 9 baking dish. Salt and pepper to taste.*

For Him: Cover baking dish and bake for 20–25 minutes at 375°. While baking, begin preparing the dessert.

A Kiss can be a comma, a question mark, or an exclamation point.

—Unknown

Glazed Apple Roll-Ups

For Him: Dip 4 crescent rolls in ¼ C. melted butter. Set aside remaining butter for the entree.

Preparation topic (take turns answering): What personality traits do you like most about me?

For Her: *Combine 1/3 C. sugar, ½ t. cinnamon, and a pinch of nutmeg. Roll buttered crescents in mixture.*

For Him: Remove skin and finely chop 1 apple. Add remaining sugar mixture. Sneak in her favorite kiss.

For Her: *Place ¼ apple in middle of each crescent. Pull corners to middle and pinch together. Bake at 350° for 20–25 minutes. Tidy up if you have time.*

Almond Chicken Crescent Entrée (cont.)

For Her: *Remove pan from oven and cover with a layer of separated (four) crescent rolls.*

For Him: Place 4 slices Swiss cheese over crescent rolls.

For Her: *Sprinkle ¼ C. sliced almonds and leftover melted butter over cheese. Set aside small amount of almonds for salad. Bake 20–25 minutes or until brown, uncovered. While baking, prepare salad.*

Kissing is a means of getting two people so close together that they can't see anything wrong with each other.

Rene Yasenek

Flavored Orange Greens

For Her: *Place you favorite lettuces on a small plate.*

For Him: Crumble blue cheese, or your favorite crumbling cheese, over top.

For Her: *Add remaining onions, slivered almonds, and water chestnuts. Open mandarin oranges and place slices on the salad and place juice in with dressing. Tease him with a little flirt.*

For Him: Mix 3 T. olive oil and 1 ½ T. sugar in small bowl. Tidy up if you have time.

For Her: *Add 1 freshly squeezed orange and 1 T. vinegar to oil mixture. Include bits of orange zest if desired. Mix together and pour desired amount over prepared salad. Salt and pepper to taste. Tidy up if you have time.*

The Dinner

Set a nice table!
Light some candles!
Sit next to each other!
Play romantic music!

"Beloved, if God so loved us, we also ought to love one another"

1 John 4:11, NKJV

Table Prayer

Dear Heavenly Father, be with us as we share this meal together. Help us build an everlasting bond as we share this meal. Let Your peace be flowing as we open our hearts in love in a new way. Bless these gifts to Your use; in Jesus' name we pray. Amen.

Be spontaneous—surprise your sweetie with a kiss or a romantic taste from your plate.

Table topics (Take Turns Answering)

1. Decide on a particular touch that will be considered your "hidden kiss." This hidden kiss can be used when you are out in public and it would not be appropriate to kiss but you cannot resist! Examples of hidden kisses are squeezing the thumb, tapping the shoulder, or a wink of the eye. Get creative! This will be a secret gesture, so only the two of you will know that it is a kiss. Decide together what your special hidden kiss will be.

2. What do you want to not change in our relationship? What are you most happy with in our relationship?

The Marriage Planner's Advice

Get to know each other's needs. It is okay if you don't agree on everything. Realize the things you do agree on and build your strengths around them. What can you do to make some of your spouse's wishes come true? Challenge yourself to do them.

Advice from other couples

Share what happens in your daily life with each other.
Take five to ten minutes each day and fill your spouse
in on what happened in your life—good or bad. Talk,
listen, listen, and listen some more. Make it a habit.
Married thirty-seven years.

Take your time to enjoy each other. When you are
finished, work together to clean the dishes.

Menu Two

Sautéed Vegetables and Steak
Peppered Provolone Bread
Heart-shaped Ice-cream Sandwiches

Special instructions to make your date great!

1. Read recipe entirely before starting.
2. Set out all your ingredients and baking dishes.
3. If only one has time to cook, both do the topics and dinner instructions.
4. If one falls behind, pitch in and help him or her.
5. Put the kids to bed, or get them a movie, so you can have time alone.

Pantry Items	Produce	Other
1 t. rosemary 1 loaf favorite herb bread Butter Pinch of salt and pepper Olive oil	½ C. carrots 1 medium onion 2 potatoes 1 green pepper 2 fresh garlic clove	Heart-shaped cookie cutter 4 soft cookies 4 scoops vanilla ice-cream Provolone cheese 1 lb. Steak

Cut out the cards below and finish the statement and place at table to be exchanged and read during dinner.

For Her
I know you love me when you...

For Him
I know you love me when you...

Kissing and Cooking

Kissing and Cooking

Sautéed Vegetables and Steak

For Him: Wash and cut 2 medium potatoes into 1-inch squares, place in 3 T. olive oil on med/high heat. Stir often. The smaller cut, the quicker it will cook.

For Her: Cut 1 medium onion and ½ C. carrots into ½-inch bite-sized pieces. Place in pan with potatoes and stir. Add two cloves of finely chopped garlic.

Preparation topic (take turns answering): When do you feel I am the most irresistible?

For Him: Cut one green pepper into bite-sized pieces and place in pan. Add rosemary (optional) and a pinch of salt and pepper. Kiss her with the heat of a hot pepper!

For Her: *Cut steak into 1-inch squares. Season it as desired. Place in pan with other vegetables until done. Continue to next recipe.*

A kiss is just a pleasant reminder that two heads are better than one.

—Unknown

Heart-shaped Ice-Cream Sandwich

For Him: Cut soft cookies with heart-shaped cookie cutter.

For Her: *Place desired amount of ice cream on the bottom cookie, then place the top cookie onto the ice cream. Put in freezer. Tickle him. (This is a fun activity to do with children.)*

Preparation Topic (take turns answering): What activity have we done together that you enjoyed the most? Set a date to do it again.

Peppered Provolone Bread

For Him: Butter both sides of bread. Place in frying pan on medium heat. Brown the bread on both sides. Kiss her while you're waiting to flip the bread.

For Her: *Place provolone cheese on browned bread. Continue cooking on medium/low heat until melted.*

For Him: Season bread with black pepper on top of melted cheese.

If you ever think of me out of the blue, just remember it's all the kisses I've blown in the air finally catching up with you.

—Christina

The Dinner

Set a nice table!
Light some candles!
Sit next to each other!
Play romantic music!

"If we live in the Spirit, let us also walk in the Spirit. Let us not become conceited, provoking one another, envying one another"

Galatians 5:25–26, NKJV

Table Prayer

Dear Heavenly Father, give us thankful hearts as we meet the day-to-day challenges of this world we live in. Help each of us to appreciate the blessings we have in each other. Open our eyes to see the blessing You have placed in our life. Bless these gifts to Your use; in Jesus' name we pray. Amen.

Be Spontaneous—give your partner a quick wink.

Table Topic (take turns answering)

1. If you could have anything at all, what would it be?

2. Just for fun get to know each other's dreams. Name three and tell why it is a dream of yours.

The Marriage Planner's Advice

After learning each other's dreams, do all you can to make them come true. Be creative and use your imagination. Drop hints from time to time so he knows you care.

Advice from Other Couples

Don't take your spouse for granted. Notice the little things she does and thank her for doing them. Challenge yourself to compliment her two or three times a week. But don't keep track to see if you are receiving compliments.

Take your time and enjoy each other. Then clean up together.

Menu Three

Sweetened Popcorn
Romantic Movie

Special instructions to make your date great!

1. Read recipe entirely before starting.
2. Set out all your ingredients and baking dishes.
3. If only one has time to cook, just pop some popcorn and do questions.
4. If one falls behind, pitch in and help him or her.
5. Put the kids to bed, or get them a movie, so you can have time alone.

Pantry Items	Produce	Other
Popcorn Puff corn (Old Dutch) Butter Oil Baking soda	Brown sugar Corn syrup	Romantic movie

Cut out the cards below and finish the statement and exchange before the movie starts.

For Her
You are my movie star because...

For Him
You are my movie star because...

Kissing and Cooking

Kissing and Cooking

For Him: Preheat oven to 325° and measure out 7 C. of puff corn and place on cookie sheet.

Preparation Topic: What is your favorite type of movie? Who are your favorite actors? What movie has touched your heart the most and why? Talk as you prepare.

For Her: *In pan place 2 T. Oil and ¼ C. popcorn on medium/high heat. Give your man a taste of the kisses to come.*

For Him: In another saucepan place ½ C. or 1 stick of butter on medium/low heat. Place popped popcorn, about 5–6 C., on cookie sheet with puffed corn.

For Her: *Add ¾ C. brown sugar and ½ C. corn syrup to butter and bring to slight boil.*

For Him: Add ½ T. baking soda. Stir as it foams up. Use large spoon. Be careful; it's very hot. *Sneak her a hot kiss when finished with this step.*

For Her: *Pour mixer over top of corns.*

For Him: Stir as she is pouring. Be careful; it is hot! Remove ¼ of mixture for tasting while the rest bakes. Feed each other; it is yummy. Place in preheated oven for 15 minutes, mixing every 5 minutes.

"Hugs and kisses are ways to express what cannot be said."

—Kacie Conroy

The Movie

Light some candles or a fire!
Grab a blanket!

And people should eat and drink and enjoy the fruits of their labor, for these are gifts from God.

Ecclesiastes 3:13 (NLT)

Movie Prayer

Dear Heavenly Father, be with us as we enjoy this time alone. Let us get to know each other on a whole new level. Open our hearts to become loving in our walk together. In Jesus' name we pray. Amen.

Movie Fun: See if you can kiss as often as they kiss in the movie And with the same passion they have in the movie. (Don't hurt each other!)

The Marriage Planner's Advice

Take this time and have a little fun with each other. Take your shoes off, put on some fuzzy slippers, and melt into each other's arms. Be in the moment, this moment, not yesterday or tomorrow.

Advice from other couples

Cuddle like there is no tomorrow. We never know for sure.

Menu Four

Creamy Mushroom-filled Ravioli with Shrimp
Sweetened Chilled Spinach
Orange Sherbet

Special instructions to make your date great!

1. Read recipe entirely before starting.
2. Set out all your ingredients and baking dishes.
3. If only one has time to cook, both do the topics
   and dinner instructions.
4. If one falls behind, pitch in and help him or her.
5. Put the kids to bed, or get them a movie, so you
   can have time alone.

Pantry Items	Produce	Other
8 T. olive oil	2 large garlic cloves	2 large chicken breasts
Grated parmesan	1 small onion	1 package pre-made
cheese, if desired	1 small red pepper	mushroom ravioli
1 T white vinegar	2 C. mushrooms	3 oz. cream cheese
2 T. brown sugar	5 C. fresh spinach	1/3 C. milk
½ t. poppy seeds		10 large or 20 small
4 T. sunflower seeds		pre-cooked, shell-less
		shrimp [or …pre-
		cooked shrimp shells
		removed]
		Orange sherbet

Cut out the cards below and finish the statement and place at the table to be exchanged and read during dinner.

For Her
You give me butterflies when...

For Him
You give me butterflies when...

Kissing and Cooking

Kissing and Cooking

Creamy Mushroom Ravioli with Shrimp

For Him: Boil 3 quarts water. Kiss her twice while waiting for water to boil. Continue to the next step.

Preparation topic (take turns answering): What would you consider a romantic weekend getaway? Think of one that is realistic and one that is a dream getaway.

For Her: *Finely chop 2 large garlic cloves and one small onion. If you tear up, ask him to kiss your tear! Set a small amount aside for salad and place remainder in a large frying pan.*

For Him: Chop one small red pepper and two cups mushrooms. Set small amount aside for salad and place remainder in pan with the other ingredients. Clean up if you have time.

For Her: *Begin cooking the ravioli in the boiling water according to the package directions. Place 3 T. oil in the frying pan with the vegetables. Heat the vegetables for three to four minutes on medium heat. Sneak him his favorite kiss. Clean up if you have time.*

For Him: Reduce the frying pan heat to low and add 3 oz. of cream cheese and 1/3 C. milk. Check on the ravioli. Drain and add to pan when finished cooking.

For Her: *Add shrimp and 2 C. fresh spinach to frying pan. Cook until shrimp is fully cooked.*

For Him: Decrease heat to very low to keep warm. Top with grated Parmesan cheese to serve.

"Kissing is like salt water. You drink, and your thirst increases."

Chinese Proverb

Chilled Sweetened Spinach

For Him: Place fresh spinach on a salad plate.

Preparation topic (take turns answering): What is a simple chore I could do to help you? Name only one and do not talk about whether you are doing it now. Do not expect it to be done consistently in the future. Only feel blessed if he or she takes the time to do it every once in a while.

For Her: *Place set-aside ingredients on top of spinach plate. Sneak him his favorite kiss. Tidy up if you have time.*

For Him: Whisk together 3 T. oil, 1 T. vinegar, 2 T. brown sugar, and ½ t. poppy seed. Pour over spinach.

For Her: *Sprinkle with 4 T. sunflower seeds.*

Orange Sherbet

For Her: *Place desired amount of sherbet in dessert dishes. Return to freezer until served.*

"Is not a kiss the very autograph of love?"
—Henry Finck

The Dinner

Set a nice table!
Light some candles!
Sit next to one another!
Play romantic music!

"Now hope does not disappoint, because the love of God has been poured out in our hearts by the Holy Spirit who was given to us"

Romans 5:5, NKJV

Table Prayer

Dear Heavenly Father, be with us as we share this meal together. Give us the wisdom to share Your love in a way that would be pleasing to You. Bless these gifts to Your use; in Jesus' name we pray. Amen.

Be spontaneous—surprise your sweetie with a kiss or a romantic taste from your plate.

Table topic (take turns answering)

1. Explain to each other what you feel you have learned most from each other.

2. Explain how it has made you a better person.

The Marriage Planner's Advice

Be sure to let each other know what you appreciate. Buy a small notebook and place it in a handy place in your bedroom. Surprise your love with a little note every once in a while. Be creative and have some fun. Keep it as an on going compliment list to each other;

view it when you need some love and encouragement and your significant other is not available.

Advice from Other Couples

Do not allow unresolved issues to go unresolved. Allow yourself a little cool-down time, but jump right back into the issue before it becomes poison. It is all right if you don't agree, but end the conversation with love."

Take your time to enjoy each other. When you are finished, work together to clean the dishes.

Menu Five

Sunset Eggs Benedict
Fresh-Fruit delight

Special instructions to make your date great!

1. Read recipe entirely before starting.
2. Set out all your ingredients and baking dishes.
3. If only one has time to cook, both do the topics and dinner instructions.
4. If one falls behind, pitch in and help him or her.
5. Put the kids to bed or get them a movie so you can have time alone.

Pantry Items	Produce	Other
Lemon juice	Eggs	Water
Salt and pepper	Fresh chives	Butter
Mayonnaise	1 apple	Canadian bacon
Sugar	1 orange	English muffins
	1 banana	
	1 tomato	

Cut out the cards below and finish the statement and place at table to be exchanged and read during dinner.

For Her
I would like to tell you...

For Him
I would like to tell you...

Kissing and Cooking

Kissing and Cooking

Fresh-Fruit Delight

For Him: Pour water into a skillet to reach a depth of 2–3 inches. Place on medium heat. Peel and slice one orange and place in bowl. Go to next step while waiting for water to boil. Kiss her while it heats up.

Preparation topic (take turns answering): Who is someone special you would like to try to visit more often? Why?

For Her: *Peel and slice one apple and place in bowl. Sneak him his favorite kiss. Tidy up if you have time.*

For Him: Peel and slice one banana and place in bowl. Add ¼ C. mayo and 2 T. sugar then stir together. Place on serving plates and refrigerate.

"When trying to get our own way, we should remember that kisses are sweeter than wine."

Unknown

Sunset Eggs Benedict

Preparation topic (take turns answering): What do you remember most about your dating days regarding hair, fun, car, other fun or funny things?

For Her: *Crack egg into a bowl and then place in hot water to poach. Do it four times. Cook for 3–5 minutes until desired firmness. Remove to paper towel. Cover to keep warm.*

For Him: Place two slices of Canadian bacon and 1 T. butter in pan on low heat.

Hollandaise Sauce

For Her: *Melt ¼ C. butter in pan over medium heat. Remove white foam. Set aside. Sneak him his favorite kiss. Clean up if you have time.*

For Him: Place cooked bacon, slice of tomato (optional), and eggs on toasted muffins she is toasting.

For Her: *Toast two divided English muffins. Place on plates. Help your honey with his last step.*

For Him: Combine one egg yolk, 1 T. cold water, and ½ T. lemon juice into very hot melted butter, whisking together while cooking over medium/low. (Use and remove from heat right away.)

For Her: *Pour hollandaise sauce over the top of eggs. Salt and pepper to taste.*

The Dinner

Set a nice table!
Light some candles!
Sit next to each other!
Play romantic music!

For I am not ashamed of the gospel of Christ, for it is the power of God to salvation for everyone who believes, for the Jew first and also for the Greek. For in it the righteousness of God is revealed from faith to faith; as it is written, "the just shall live by faith"

Romans 1:16–17, NKJV

Table Prayer

Dear Heavenly Father, be with us as we share this meal together. Help us by the power of the Holy Spirit to live by faith. Help us love each other in a way that would be pleasing to You. Bless these gifts to your use; in Jesus' name we pray. Amen.

Be spontaneous—give a quick smile or wink.

Table Topic (take turns answering)

1. What are some things you would like to do together alone?

2. When would be the best time for both of you?

164

Make two dates? One she would like and one he would like.

The Marriage Planner's Advice

We are all individuals, so we like to do different things. Be considerate and enjoy doing something your spouse would like to do (love it just because your loved one loves it). Do it because you love her, not because you love the activity. Enjoy your spouse enjoying him or herself.

Advice from Other Couples

"Make marriage simple, love without so many conditions!"

Take your time to enjoy each other. When you are finished, work together to clean the dishes.

Menu Six

Philly Steak Delight
Heavenly Potatoes
Chilled Tomato salad
Chocolate Mint Ice Cream

Special instructions to make your date great!

1. Read recipe entirely before starting.
2. Set out all your ingredients and baking dishes.
3. If only one has time to cook, both do the topics
   and dinner instructions.
4. If one falls behind, pitch in and help him or her.
5. Put the kids to bed, or get them a movie, so you
   can have time alone.

Pantry Items	Produce	Other
Olive oil	2 medium potatoes	Butter
Flour	Chives	Italian or hoagie buns
Salt and pepper	Onion	Cheddar cheese
	Green bell pepper	Sour cream
	2 Tomatoes	¾ lb. steak
		4 slices mozzarella cheese
		Cottage cheese
		Chocolate mint ice cream

Cut out the cards below and finish the statement and place at table to be exchanged and read during dinner.

For Her
Love means this to me...

For Him
Love means this to me...

Kissing and Cooking

Kissing and Cooking

Heavenly Potatoes

For Him: Wash 2 medium potatoes and pierce with a fork. Rub with olive oil and salt. Place in microwave for 2-minute increments until done. Pre-heat oven to 325°. Go to next step. Kiss her twice while your potatoes are cooking.

Preparation topic (take turns answering): Explain to me when I am most desirable to you?

For Her: *Combine 2 T. butter 1 T. flour, 2 T. sour cream, and 1/3 C. cheddar cheese. Tidy up if you have time.*

For Him: Chop ¼ C. chives and place with her mixture. Save a small amount for top of potatoes and tomato salad.

For Her: *When potatoes are done, remove ½ of insides of potatoes and combine it with above mixture. Place mixture back into potato and place in the oven to warm. Give him his favorite kiss.*

"If a kiss could say just how I love you, my lips would be on yours forever!"

—Anonymous

Chilled Tomato Salad

For Him: Wash and remove the stem from the tomatoes. Cut open with and *x* mark. Tidy up if you have time.

Preparation topic (take turns answering): If we were locked in a room for ten hours, what would you want to do to pass the time?

For Her: *Place ¼ C. cottage cheese inside of tomato and top with set-aside chives. Salt and pepper to taste. Kiss him lightly on his neck. Tidy up if you have time.*

Chocolate Chip Mint Ice Cream

For Him: Place Ice cream in small dessert bowls. Place in freezer until served. Kiss her like you need warmed up after handling the cold dessert.

Philly Steak Delights

For Him: Thinly slice 1 small onion.
For Her: Slice one small green pepper.
For Him: Heat 3 T. olive oil in skillet at medium/ high heat. Place the onions and bell pepper into a pan. Stirring occasionally until desired doneness. Place on one half of the skillet.
For Her: Thinly slice steak and place in one half of skillet until done to desired taste. Mix together when done. Salt and pepper to taste.

For him: Spoon onto buns and place slices of cheese on top. Place in oven for 5 minutes. Serve with choice of condiments.

"If your spouse doesn't share their kisses, share yours with him!"

—Kim Reutzel

The Dinner

Set a nice table!
Light some candles!
Sit next to each other!
Play romantic music!

"For God has not given us a spirit of fear, but of power and of love and of a sound mind"

2 Timothy 1:7, NKJV

Table Prayer

Dear Heavenly Father, be with us as we share this meal together. We love how You have made us each different and with special gifts. Please help us understand each other so we can be a blessing to You and each other. Help us to be patient with each other when we do not see eye to eye. Bless these gifts to Your use; in Jesus' name we pray. Amen.

Be spontaneous—surprise your sweetie with a kiss or a romantic taste from your plate.

Table Topic (take turns answering)

1. How do you think you are different and alike?

2. How does the above help or hurt your relationship?

The Marriage Planner's Advice

God made each of you with different temperaments to fulfill his plan for you in his life. Many of your differences are caused by your differences. It is important to remember your opinions are just that—

opinions. Allow your spouse the room to be himself or herself; try to love her the way God made her. Always try to compromise, and if that doesn't work, just simply agree to disagree in the name of love.

Advice from Other Couples

Accept each other the way you are. Try and try, and then try harder. Married forty-one years.

Take your time to enjoy each other. When you are finished, work together to clean up.

Menu Seven

Creamy Chicken Enchiladas
Crispy Iceberg Salad
Grilled Chocolate Tortillas

Special instructions to make your date great!

1. Read recipe entirely before starting.
2. Set out all your ingredients and baking dishes.
3. If only one has time to cook, both do the topics and dinner instructions.
4. If one falls behind, pitch in and help him or her.
5. Put the kids to bed, or get them a movie, so you can have time alone.

Pantry Items	Produce	Other
¼ t. cinnamon	2 C. broccoli or 1 C.	1 lb. chicken
1 pinch nutmeg	green pepper	10.5 oz. cream of
1 T. brown sugar	1 jalapeno pepper (opt.)	chicken soup
Cooking spray	2 medium tomatoes	Chopped almonds
Olive oil	1 small onion	8 oz. Colby-Jack
½ C. small marshmal-	1 head iceberg lettuce	cheese
lows		8 oz. sour cream
Favorite salad dressing		10 large flour tortilla shells
Almonds		½ C. sliced black olives
		(opt.)
		½ C. chocolate chips

Cut out the cards below and finish the statement in writing. Place at table to be exchanged and read during dinner.

For Her
I like it most when you kiss...

For Him
I like it most when you kiss...

Kissing and Cooking

Kissing and Cooking

Creamy Chicken Enchiladas

For Him: Begin boiling chicken in 2 ½ C. of water over medium/high heat. Give her a little back rub while the chicken is cooking. Move to next step.

Preparation topic (take turns answering): Pick three couples you would like to double date with. (Make sure you pick couples that would be a positive influence on your relationship.) Think of three things you could do on your double date.

For Her: *Preheat oven to 375°. Finely chop one small onion. Kiss him if you tear up. Set a small amount aside for the salad, if desired, and place the rest in a large mixing bowl. Tidy up if you have time.*

For Him: Finely chop 1 C. green pepper and/or 2 C. broccoli and place in bowl with onions. Set a small amount aside for salad. Did she tear up? If she did she owes you a kiss.

For Her: *Slice two tomatoes into bite-sized cubes. Set aside for topping enchiladas and salad. Give him his favorite kiss. Finely chop 1 jalapeño, if desired, and place in the bowl with the onions and broccoli.*

For Him: Remove chicken from boiling water and cut into bite-sized pieces to expedite the cooking process. Return the cut chicken pieces to the boiling water if not done.

For Her: *Place one can cream of chicken, 8 oz. sour cream, and 1 ½ C. Colby-Jack cheese into the bowl with the other ingredients. Tidy up if you have time.*

For Him: When chicken is fully cooked, place in the large mixing bowl with the rest of the ingredients. Tidy up if you have time. Maybe nibble on her ear.

Both: Place ½ C. of the mixture into one of the flour tortilla shells. Roll the shell into a tube and place in a 9 x 13-inch pan. Do the same with seven other tortillas and place them side by side in the pan. Place any leftover mixture on top. Place uncovered in oven for 20 minutes.

For Him: Slice ½ C. black olives, if desired.

For Her: *When enchiladas are finished, top them with the remaining cheese, ¾ of the chopped tomato, and the sliced olives. Top each enchilada with a dollop of sour cream if desired.*

"Happiness is like a kiss—it feels best when you give it to someone else."

Author unknown

Crispy Iceberg Salad

For Him: Cut one head iceberg lettuce in half, then cut that half into two pieces. Place one piece on each of two salad plates.

For Her: *Place set-aside onions, pepper and/or broccoli, and tomato on top of lettuce. Top with your favorite dressing. Place chopped almonds on top as desired.*

Preparation topic (take turns answering): In what ways would you like me to compliment you more?

Grilled Chocolate Tortillas

For Him: Spray one side of two tortilla shells with cooking spray and place on cookie sheet.

For Her: *Mix 1 T. brown sugar, ¼ t. cinnamon, and a pinch of nutmeg. Sprinkle on sprayed side of shells.*

For Him: Place ½ C. chocolate chips, ½ C. mini marshmallows, and 1 T. chopped almonds on unsprayed side of shell, then top with other shell, leaving the sugar mixture on the outside. Place in warm oven until crispy. Turn off oven, but keep inside oven until ready to serve. Using a pizza cutter, cut tortilla into eight slices. If you have time finish, your backrub and ask for one in return. Maybe a little kiss on the neck also.

"Love is like a balloon. It continues to grow as long as you put something into it."

—Kim Reutzel

The Dinner

Set a nice table!
Light some candles!
Sit next to each other!
Play romantic music!

"Be strong and of good courage, do not fear nor be afraid of them; for the LORD your God, He is the one who goes with you. He will not leave you nor forsake you"

Deuteronomy 31:6, NKJV

Table Prayer

Dear Heavenly Father, be with us as we share this meal together. Help us to be strong in our marriage, knowing You are always with us during good times or bad. Let Your light shine in us to brighten each other's days. Bless these gifts to Your use; in Jesus' name we pray. Amen.

Be spontaneous—hold hands or kiss between bites.

Table Topic (take turns answering)

Would you rather have a bath with candles or a back rub with candles?

How would you like me to flirt with you? In public? In private?

The Marriage Planner's Advice

You will have good and bad times in your marriage. Remember during the bad times, that too will pass. It may seem very hard, but hang in there, and you'll reap the blessing later. Some of your greatest growing together is done during the hard times.

Advice from Other Couples

I always thought I had things so bad when I was married. I did not appreciate what I had. The saying is true, you don't always know what you have until it's gone. Don't make the same mistake I did. I can't repair my mistake. Divorced.

Take your time to enjoy each other. When you are finished, work together to clean up.

Menu Eight

Sunny Island Kabobs
Kiwi Surprise
Buttery Garlic Bread

Special instructions to make your date great!

1. Read recipe entirely before starting.
2. Set out all your ingredients and baking dishes.
3. If only one has time to cook, both do the topics and dinner instructions.
4. If one falls behind, pitch in and help him or her.
5. Put the kids to bed, or get them a movie, so you can have time alone.

Pantry Items	Produce	Other
Salt and pepper One loaf wheat bread ¼ t. garlic salt ½ T. olive oil ½ T. white vinegar 1 can pineapple (chunked) 1 can mandarin oranges	1 large onion 1 large tomato 1 lime 1 orange 1 head of favorite lettuce 2 kiwi	4 skewers 10 large or 20 small shrimp Barbeque sauce, if desired Butter

Cut out the cards below and finish the statement and place at table to be exchanged and read during dinner.

For Her
I shiver when you...

For Him
I shiver when you...

Kissing and Cooking

Kissing and Cooking

Sunny Island Kabobs

For Him: Start and prepare grill or skillet. Cut one
           large onion into large pieces. Place a small
           amount aside for kiwi salad. Kiss her like
           it is your first kiss.

Preparation topic (take turns answering): What
would mean more to you, listening to each other for
a half hour or hugging and kissing for a half hour?
Why do you pick that? What is your favorite subject
to talk about? Name two.

For Her: *Slice one large tomato into eighths. Soak
            wooden skewer in water. Kiss him if he tears
            up.*
For Him: Clean and prepare shrimp or other desired
           meat.
For Her: *Open the can of pineapple chunks. Drain
            juice in a cup and set aside for salad. Give
            him his favorite kiss.*
Both: Place   shrimp,   onion,   tomato,   and

pineapples on skewers in random order. Tidy up if you have time. Salt and pepper to taste. Continue with salad for marinade ingredients to sprinkle over kabobs and salad.

"Her lips on his could tell him better than her stumbling words."

—Margaret Mitchell

Kiwi Surprise

For Him: Open Mandarin oranges and strain juice in cup with pineapple juice.

For Her: *Peel and slice two kiwis. Give him a fruity kiss.*

For Him: Place favorite lettuce on salad plates. Place mandarin oranges, kiwi, and onions on top of lettuce.

For Her: *Combine the pineapple and mandarin juices with the juice from one fresh squeezed orange. Separate the juice in half. Add 1 ½ T. olive oil and ½ T. vinegar to salad juices. Pour over salad. Salt and pepper to taste.*

Sunny Island Kabobs

For Him: Sprinkle kabob's with other half of juices. Cut one lime in half and sprinkle the kabobs with the juice of that lime.

Both: Place kabobs on grill. Cook 15 minutes or until cooked thoroughly.

Preparation topic (take turns answering): In what ways would you like me to compliment you more? What things do you do that you feel go un-noticed?

Buttery Garlic Bread

For Him: Butter both sides of sliced wheat bread. Sprinkle one side with a small amount of garlic salt. Brown each side on a frying pan or grill.

"Love unconditionally, argue conditionally."
—Kim Reutzel

The Dinner

Set a nice table!
Light some candles!
Sit next to each other!
Play romantic music!

"For by grace you have been saved through faith, and that not of yourselves; it is the gift of God, not of works, lest anyone should boast"

Ephesians 2:8–9, NKJV

Table Prayer

Dear Heavenly Father, be with us as we share this meal together. Please allow us to know and cherish our blessings hidden in our lives as husband and wife. Reveal to us the special gifts we each have that bring happiness into our family. Bless these gifts to Your use; in Jesus' name we pray. Amen.

Be spontaneous—kiss, smile, and laugh.

Table Topic (take turns answering)

1. What are some things that are hard to talk about with me? (Be sensitive to each other's feelings.) Why is it hard?

2. If you were to describe me to someone who doesn't know me yet, what would you tell him or her?

The Marriage Planner's Advice

Be sure to tell each other your feelings. You do not have to understand your spouse's feelings—just listen. Taking time to listen is the start to understanding and a sure road to letting her know you care.

Advice from Other Couples

During arguments, don't yell back and forth—that doesn't get you anywhere. Take a few minutes to cool down and discuss the issue when you are not so heated up. Married fifteen years.

Take your time to enjoy each other. When you are finished, clean up together.

Menu Nine

Tomato Dip with Chips
Cheesy Zucchini and Rice
Banana Creamed Pie

Special instructions to make your date great!

1. Read recipe entirely before starting.
2. Set out all your ingredients and baking dishes.
3. If only one has time to cook, both do the topics and dinner instructions.
4. If one falls behind, pitch in and help him or her.
5. Put the kids to bed, or get them a movie, so you can have time alone.

Pantry Items	Produce	Other
Salt and pepper	Zucchini (1 lg. or 2	1 lb. hamburger
Rice (quick cooking)	small)	1 pkg. cheddar cheese
Sugar	Large onion	Pie crust
White Vinegar	2 bananas	Banana instant pud-
Cream of mushroom	Parsley or cilantro	ding
soup	Jalapeno pepper (opt.)	Cool Whip
	Tomato	Cottage cheese
		Nacho chips

Cut out the cards below and finish the statement and place at table to be exchanged and read during dinner.

For Her
I thank God for you because...

For Him
I thank God for you because...

Kissing and Cooking

Kissing and Cooking

"I can't read lips unless they're touching mine."

—Jon Troast

Cheesy Zucchini and Rice

For Him: Preheat oven to 350. Cook rice as directed on package. Move to next step, but keep an eye on the rice. Surprise her with a kiss sometime while this is cooking. Tidy up if you have time. Keep oven on.

Preparation topic (take turns answering): If I were to go on a long vacation, what would you miss most about me?

For Her: *Brown hamburger in a skillet until done. Move to next item but keep an eye on the hamburger, stirring occasionally.*

For Him: Slice zucchini and onion then place in microwave dish. Set aside half of onions. Heat in microwave until tender (about

3–5 minutes). Give her a tender kiss on her hand.

For Her: *Open cream of mushroom soup and 1 ½ C. cheddar and 1 C. Cottage cheese and place in a bowl.*

For Him: Add cooked rice, zucchini, and hamburger to bowl and lightly stir. Put in 9 x 13 sprayed baking pan and place in oven for 20 minutes or until bubbling.

Tomato Dip with Chips

For Him: Preheat oven as directed on piecrust. Place in oven and set timer for directed time. Chunk tomato and place in a bowl.

Preparation topic (take turns answering):

1. What are the things I do or say that make you feel protected in our marriage?

2. What do I do or say that make you feel close to me?

For Her: *Finely chop rest of onion and place in a bowl with the tomato.*

For Him: Place 1 T. sugar and 1 T. vinegar in bowl. Then give her a kiss as warm as the oven is.

For Her: *Cut cilantro or parsley and finely chop jalapeno peppers, then stir together in bowl. Serve with chips while preparing meal. Enjoy!*

Banana Cream Pie

For Him: Slice banana to be placed in pudding mixture. Save a few slices for top of Cool Whip.

For Her: *Prepare pudding as directed on package. Pour pudding and bananas in piecrust and top with Cool Whip. Refrigerate until served.*

"A slow kiss can melt away built-up tension."
—Kim Reutzel

The Dinner

Set a nice table!
Light some candles!
Sit next to each other!
Play romantic music!

"Judge not, and you shall not be judged. Condemn not, and you shall not be condemned. Forgive, and you will be forgiven"

Luke 6:37, NKJV

Table Prayer

Dear Heavenly Father, be with us as we share this meal together. Help us to not judge and condemn each other. Put Your Spirit of forgiveness into our hearts so we may forgive as you have forgiven us. Bless these gifts to your use; in Jesus' name we pray. Amen.

Be spontaneous—kiss, smile, and laugh.

Table Topic (take turns answering)

Look over the tool: conflict to compromise. Use this tool when you have differences. How do you feel this could help in times of conflict? Agree to use this when needed.

The Marriage Planner's Advice

Conflict is a given. Two people cannot live so close together and not have a disagreement from time to time. Sometimes it is very difficult to come to an agreement. If you have a disagreement that has gone unresolved, seek professional advice.

Advice from Other Couples

Things may seem like a big deal that really are not. Do not let something fester so long that it separates the two of you. The grass is not always greener on the other side. Think long and hard about your stubbornness. I wish I had. Divorced.

Take your time to enjoy each other. When you are finished, work together to clean up.

Menu Ten

Cheesy Chicken Manicotti
Sweet Slaw
Seasoned Custard

Special instructions to make your date great!

1. Read recipe entirely before starting.
2. Set out all your ingredients and baking dishes.
3. If only one has time to cook, both do the topics and dinner instructions.
4. If one falls behind, pitch in and help him or her.
5. Put the kids to bed, or get them a movie, so you can have time alone.

Pantry Items	Produce	Other
Salt and pepper	1 small red onion	1 lb. Chicken
2/3 C. sugar	1 small head of cabbage	½ C. mayonnaise
2 t. white vinegar	1 large garlic clove	1 box manicotti noodles
½ t. vanilla		3 eggs
Large sealable plastic		½ C. cottage cheese
bag		½ C. parmesan cheese
Pinch nutmeg		½ C. sour cream
Pinch cinnamon		2 C. milk
Cooking spray		8 oz. mozzarella cheese
		12-16 oz. spaghetti sauce
		8 oz. cream cheese

Cut out the cards below and finish the statement and place at table to be exchanged and read during dinner.

For Her
One romantic thing you do is...

For Him
One romantic thing you do is...

Kissing and Cooking

Kissing and Cooking

Cheesy Chicken Manicotti

For Him: Prepare manicotti noodles according to box directions. Continue to next step.

Preparation topic (take turns answering): If your life and marriage were the plot for a movie or book, what do you think it would be about? Would it be a romance, comedy, thriller, or scary movie? Why?

For Her: Boil chicken in 3 C. of water until cooked thoroughly. Preheat oven to 350°. Continue on to next step but keep an eye on the chicken. Kiss your honey. Move on to next recipe…

Seasoned Custard

For Him: Spray custard dishes (or small oven-safe dishes) with cooking spray and set in baking dish. The smaller the dish the quicker it will be done.

For Her: *Beat 3 eggs in a large bowl. Add ½ t. vanilla and 1/3 C. sugar. Beat until dissolved.*

For Him: Warm 2 C. milk in a pan until hot. Give her a slow, warm kiss as this is warming. Mix warm milk into mixture above until blended. Sprinkle cinnamon and nutmeg over top of custard.

For Her: *Place the custard dishes in an empty baking pan. Fill the baking pan with hot water, avoiding getting water in the custard dishes, until the bottom half of the custard dish is submerged in water. Fill custard dishes with mixture to the water level. Place in oven for 35–45 minutes, depending on the size of your custard dishes. (Custard will be firm when done.)*

"Kisses blown are kisses wasted. Kisses are not kisses unless they are tasted."

—Jill Zebby

For Him: Place 8 oz. cream cheese, ½ C. cottage cheese, ½ C. parmesan cheese, and ½ cup sour cream in a bowl. Tidy up if you have time.

For Her: *Cut chicken into bite-sized pieces and place into bowl with cheeses and sour cream. Tidy up if you have time. Give him a little kiss.*

For Him: Finely chop 1 large garlic clove and 1 small onion. Set a small amount of onion aside for slaw and place the rest in a bowl. Mix all bowl ingredients. Place the contents of the bowl in a strong plastic sealable bag. With scissors cut off a very small portion of the corner of the bag. Using the cut corner, carefully squeeze contents of the bag into cooked manicotti noodles. Place the filled noodles in sprayed baking dish. Ask your sweetie to help you with this.

For Her: *Pour spaghetti sauce and mozzarella over dish and place in oven for 20–30 or until boiling. Tidy up if you have time. Check on custard.*

Preparation topic (take turns answering): Would you rather have me give you a compliment or buy you a gift? Why?

Sweet Slaw

For Him: Cut head of cabbage into 1-inch slices and place in a bowl.

For Her: *Place leftover chopped onion in bowl with cabbage. Add 2 t. vinegar, ½ C. mayonnaise and ¼ C. sugar and mix. Pour over top of cabbage and toss. You may have time to give each other a foot massage. Enjoy!*

"When love is found, care for it so it is not lost."

—Kim Reutzel

The Dinner

Set a nice table!
Light some candles!
Sit next to each other!
Play romantic music!

"Trust in the LORD with all your heart; do not depend on your own understanding. Seek his will in all you do and he will direct your path"
Proverbs 3:5–6, NLT

Table Prayer

Dear Heavenly Father, be with us as we share this meal together and help us to Trust in You while we trust each other. Help us to understand the path You have for our lives. Bless these gifts to your use; in Jesus' name we pray. Amen.

Be spontaneous—use your imaginations!

Table Topic (take turns answering)

How do you find it hard to trust each other? Other people? God?

The Marriage Planner's Advice

The above Bible verse is truly a lifesaver for me. When I don't know what else to do, I remember to: 1) trust God. 2) Don't try to understand. 3) Seek his will in prayer. 4) The verse says he *will* direct your path, not he *may* direct your path. So take one step at a time, trusting God is there with you, without allowing any room for doubt.

Advice from Other Couples

Life is very hard, and you don't know what is going to happen tomorrow. Build your trust in God first and then in each other. Build trust one step at a time. The first step is to decide to be trustworthy, and then start doing the things a trustworthy spouse does. Married twenty-four years.

Take your time to enjoy each other. When you are finished, work together to clean

Menu Eleven

Cheese and Crackers
Picnic Turkey Wraps
Creamy Marshmallow and Strawberries

Special instructions to make your date great!

1. Read recipe entirely before starting.
2. Set out all your ingredients and baking dishes.
3. If only one has time to cook, both do the topics and dinner instructions.
4. If one falls behind, pitch in and help him or her.
5. Get a babysitter for the kids, if possible.

Pantry Items	Produce	Other
Salt and pepper	Avocado	Sliced turkey
Favorite crackers	Lettuce	Spinach wraps (or
Kettle chips	Onion	other)
	Strawberries	Sliced Swiss cheese
		Cream cheese
		Marshmallow cream
		Chunked cheese (2
		kinds)

Cut out the cards below and finish the statement and place at table to be exchanged and read during dinner.

For Her
When I look into your eyes...

For Him
When I look into your eyes...

Kissing and Cooking

Kissing and Cooking

Cheese and Crackers

For Him: Cut cheese and place in bag or container, then place into picnic basket along with crackers.

Preparation topic (take turns answering): Where would you like to go for our picnic? A park, lake, field, car, or comfortably sit in front of the fireplace; or any other special place?

Picnic Turkey Wraps

For Him: Spread cream cheese on inside of 2 wraps. Get her excited about your date with a kiss.

For Her: Peel and cut avocado into small pieces and place on cream cheese.

For Him: Cut onion and place desired amount on wraps.

Both: Place lettuce, Swiss cheese, and turkey on wrap. Salt and pepper to taste. Roll up and place in bag or storage container and place in basket.

"You may conquer with the sword, but you are conquered by a kiss."

—Daniel Heinsius

Creamy Marshmallow and Strawberries

For Him: Wash and dry strawberries and place in a container, then put them in the basket. Give her a sweet little kiss. Tidy up.

For Her: *Mix together leftover cream and equal amount of marshmallow cream. Place in container and then in basket. Tidy up.*

For Him: Place chips in basket and grab something to drink and a blanket to sit on. Set off to your decided destination. Don't forget the basket, book, and your partner!

The Picnic

Lay out the blanket.
Sit next to each other!

Be anxious for nothing, but in everything by prayer and supplication, with thanksgiving, let your requests be made known to God; and the peace of God, which surpasses all understanding, will guard your hearts and minds through Christ Jesus.

Philemon 4:6–7 (NLT)

Table Prayer

Dear Heavenly Father, be with us as we share this picnic together. Let us experience life outside our normal surroundings with excitement. Teach us to relax and fall deeper in love with each other. Bless these gifts to your use; in Jesus' name we pray. Amen.

Be spontaneous—use your imaginations.

Picnic Topic (take turns answering)

What are some other things you would like to do that we do not take the time to do together? Name two and set up a time to do them.

The Marriage Planner's Advice

We get stuck doing the same things over and over again. Life becomes unexciting. Try to put the more important things in your life before less important things. It is not always easy because the demands we have on our time are so obvious. Yet it is important to spend time alone to have a flourishing and loving relationship.

Advice from Other Couples

Life is so busy. You start to live on autopilot. Make special time to keep your relationship fresh. If you don't, your marriage can suffer. Married ten years.

Take your time and enjoy each other.

Menu Twelve

Rolled Lasagna with Veggies
French Baguette
Creamy Cucumbers over Spinach
Chilled Chocolate Fudge Pie

Special instructions to make your date great!

1. Read recipe entirely before starting.
2. Set out all your ingredients and baking dishes.
3. If only one has time to cook, both do the topics
    and dinner instructions.
4. If one falls behind, pitch in and help him or her.
5. Put the kids to bed, or get them a movie, so you
    can have time alone.

Pantry Items	Produce	Other
Salt and pepper	1 cucumber	1 lb. hamburger
Sugar	2 C. spinach	8 lasagna noodles
White Vinegar	Red onion	8 oz. mozzarella cheese
Mayo or salad dress-ing	1 green pepper and/or	1 C. cottage cheese
	2/3 C. broccoli	1 can spaghetti sauce
Cooking spray	3 basil leaves	1 large egg
French baguette	2 garlic clove	Whipped topping
Butter	1 tomato	Chocolate fudge pudding
		Graham cracker pie curst
		1 ¾ C. milk

Cut out the cards below and finish the statement and place at table to be exchanged and read during dinner.

For Her
I am better today because...

For Him
I am better today because...

Kissing and Cooking

Kissing and Cooking

Rolled Lasagna with Veggies and French Baguette

Both: Cut bread and rub peeled garlic clove over slices, then butter to taste and place on cookie sheet.

For Him: Cook 8 lasagna noodles according to package directions. Preheat oven to 385°. Keep an eye on noodles and continue to next steps.

Preparation topic (take turns answering): I have self-doubt about these things in my life. Name two. You could help me with these things by doing what?

For Her: Brown hamburger in frying pan and place in mixing bowl. Continue to next steps, but keep an eye on the hamburger. Help each other when needed.

For Him: Finally chop ½ of onion and ½ of green pepper and/or broccoli then place in bowl. Cut the other half of onion in large pieces and set aside for cucumber salad. Lightly stir noodles. Kiss her like you love her more than life itself.

For Her: *Finally chop tomato, basil leaves and garlic clove then place in bowl. Open your favorite spaghetti sauce. Stir in hamburger. Spray the 9 x 13 inch baking dish. Drain meat and noodles when finished cooking.*

For Him: Place 1 C. cottage cheese, 1 C. spaghetti sauce, 1 C. mozzarella cheese, and one beaten egg in bowl. Stir contents of bowl mixture.

Both: Place mixture on lasagna noodle topping with 4 spinach leaves (repeat seven times). Roll each noodle one by one and place individually in sprayed baking dish. Top with remainder of mixture, spaghetti sauce, and cheese. Place in pre-heated oven for 30–40 minutes or until bubbling.

"When we give love to someone, we are giving away one of our most valuable possessions."
—Kim Reutzel

Chilled Chocolate Fudge Pie

For Him: Place pudding mix in shakable container. Add 1 ¾ C. milk and shake for 2 minutes. Make sure lid is on tight. Give her a sweet little kiss. Tidy up.

For Her: Add 1 C. whipped topping to container and shake for another 2 minutes, then place in graham cracker pie crust. Place in freezer until ready to cut and serve. Tidy up.

Preparation topic (take turns answering): What could we do for someone else (donation of time or money) that would make us feel good as a family? Choose two things, and set times to do them. Try to get at least one of these things done within the next month. Work together as a family to do these projects.

Creamy Cucumber over Spinach

For Him: Peel and slice cucumber and place in a bowl. Help your honey with her next job.

For Her: Combine ½ C. mayo or salad dressing, 2 ½ T. vinegar and 2 ½ T. sugar. Add mixture to the cucumbers and set aside onions. Place 20–30 spinach leaves on a plate and top with cucumber salad. Salt and pepper to taste. Give him a kiss for a job well done.

"A loving kiss is a gift given straight from the heart."

—Kim Reutzel

The Dinner

Set a nice table.
Light some candles.
Sit next to each other!
"So let each one give as he purposes in his heart,

not grudgingly or of necessity; for God loves a cheerful giver"

2 Corinthians 9:7, NKJV

Table Prayer

Dear Heavenly Father, be with us as we share this dinner. Help each of us to be a gracious giver not only to each other but to others you place in our lives. As we give to others, place thankfulness into our hearts for the gifts You have given us. Bless these gifts to your use; in Jesus' name we pray. Amen.

Be spontaneous—flirt with each other.

Table Topic (take turns answering)

What do you feel God has blessed you with? Name three things. Do you feel everything you have is a gift from God? What are some of your gifts that you could share with others? How have others blessed you with their gifts?

The Marriage Planner's Advice

When you are feeling down, count your blessings. Even when things are not going well, you can always find something that has. Don't allow yourself to stay in a state of depression, but rather make yourself be a blessing to you by having a thankful heart. If you have a hard time doing this, then simply find someone to help that is in need. Get your mind off yourself and onto someone else. Your spouse might be this someone else, so start with him or her.

Advice from Other Couples

Commit to a daily kiss. Morning, day, or night, it doesn't matter when, just make it an important part of the day. Married fifty-two years

Take your time and enjoy each other, then clean up together!

Contact Info

Kim M. Reutzel
3008 120th Ave, PO Box 42
Burt, IA 50522
515–924–3851
email: kim@kimreutzel.com
webpage: www.kissingandcooking.com

e|LIVE

listen|imagine|view|experience

AUDIO BOOK DOWNLOAD INCLUDED WITH THIS BOOK!

In your hands you hold a complete digital entertainment package. Besides purchasing the paper version of this book, this book includes a free download of the audio version of this book. Simply use the code listed below when visiting our website. Once downloaded to your computer, you can listen to the book through your computer's speakers, burn it to an audio CD or save the file to your portable music device (such as Apple's popular iPod) and listen on the go!

How to get your free audio book digital download:

1. Visit www.tatepublishing.com and click on the e|LIVE logo on the home page.
2. Enter the following coupon code:
   d1e0-df86-0b2e-cd96-5758-74b6-5e9d-ed07
3. Download the audio book from your e|LIVE digital locker and begin enjoying your new digital entertainment package today!